TIMES PAST 2

EVERY PICTURE TELLS A STORY . . .

More evocative images from the archives of the *Herald* and *Ev*

D0262714

Words by Russell Leadbetter

Picture Editing by Rod Sibbald

BLACK & WHITE PUBLISHING

First published 2006

by Black & White Publishing Ltd,

99 Giles Street, Edinburgh EH6 6BZ

ISBN 13: 9 781 84502 1160

ISBN 10: 184502 116 9

British Library Cataloguing in publication data: a catalogue record for
this book is available from The British Library.

Printed and bound in Poland

www.polskabook.pl

These photos, which are drawn from the *Evening Times* partwork 'TimesPast' and the *Picture This* exhibition can be
purchased from the front counter at Newsquest (Glasgow), 200 Renfield Street, Glasgow G2 3QB, tel: 0141 302 6015

Acknowledgements: Additional picture research by
Malcolm Beaton, Jim McNeish, Tony Murray and Eva Mutter

Contents

1. GROWING UP   2

2. ENTERTAINMENT   16

3. THAT'S LIFE   24

4. HEALTH   40

5. AERIAL   52

6. NEWSPAPERS   64

7. MORE ENTERTAINMENT   76

8. THE FOG   88

9. ON THE MOVE   100

10. PEOPLE POWER   112

11. FOOTBALL FANS   124

12. DANCING   136

13. CHRISTMAS   146

'Should I throw this one away?' Children fish for tiddlers in Queen's Park pond, Glasgow, July 1947. Fishing was a great way to pass the summer holidays for many Glasgow youngsters. Sometimes their pet dog came along too.
Photographer: Chris McCrae

GROWING UP

CHAPTER ONE

GROWING UP

When the *Picture This* exhibition was held in Glasgow at the beginning of 2006, there were more than one hundred photographs on display. The one that seemed to attract most interest was also the one that best summed up the occasional miseries and uncertainties of childhood. It shows a little boy lost being spoken to by a kindly policeman. What stirred pity among the exhibition visitors some fifty years after the picture was taken was the boy's appearance – the tousled hair, the ill-fitting shorts, the bare legs, the gym shoes on the wrong feet and a sense of bewilderment that was plain for all to see. The boy had become separated from his parents in Edinburgh's Princes Street, which was full of tourists at the time. For a while, he took in some of the sights on his own (not having much of a choice) but a friendly stranger advised him to take shelter within some scaffolding, whereupon a crowd gathered and stared at the wee boy. (*The Bulletin*, in its mini photo-essay on the boy, carried a picture of him behind a barrier, being gazed upon by amused passers-by as if he were a faintly exotic zoo attraction.) A passing policeman intervened and tried to get some words out of the boy. Eventually, by means not recorded, the parents came upon the scene and reclaimed their son.

In fact, few of the pictures in the exhibition – or, for that matter, in the whole *Evening Times/Herald* archive – are as affecting as those that feature children, whether (as here) they're building a Guy Fawkes bonfire or weeping on their first day at a new primary school. Another one in this section, taken outside a newly opened milk bar in Cowcaddens, shows local kids enjoying the spectacle. Not many of them would have too much to look forward to in their daily lives in Glasgow in the 1930s.

That said, children's welfare was an unwavering priority in a city that had more than its share of overcrowding and the illnesses that could flourish in such conditions. According to historian Irene Maver, in the 1890s, James Burn Russell, the city's first full-time Medical Officer of Health, used the poor state of Glasgow's children's health as a polemical device to agitate for a better public environment. More parks in working-class areas, he believed, could remedy the ill health and the anti-social behaviour that stemmed from youngsters' excessive confinement. The overcrowding was of grimly epic proportions. In 1888, Maver says, one in five babies born in slums died before reaching its first birthday.

Medical and public health officials made gradual progress in tackling childhood illnesses, with improvements frequently being observed in official statistics. At 22.4 per 1000 of the population, the birth rate was the highest on record and infant and maternal mortalities were falling.

The common infectious diseases of childhood continued to decline. Deaths from scarlet fever had dropped from 102 in 1932 to a record low of one in 1946. Deaths from diphtheria, however, remained a problem – 226 deaths in 1940 and thirty-nine in 1946. But, by 1954, there was only one recorded death from diphtheria.

In a five-day-long series on Glasgow's children in 1957, the *Evening Times* could report that the under-fives 'are growing healthier every year'. In 1900, it said, 2754 children aged between one and five had died. In 1954, that number had dropped to ninety-two. 'This striking improvement,' said the paper's venerable writer Meg Munro, 'is due to the rise in the standard of living and child care and is a long-term result of Glasgow's child welfare and allied services.' Each year, the city spent more than £12 million on educational services and more than £30,000 on maternity and child welfare. Antenatal clinics had been set up across Glasgow and in the new housing schemes that were being built on the city's outskirts at the time.

The Corporation had also come up with various projects to aid children. Those who, thanks to poor housing conditions, were denied sunshine, light and fresh air attended ultraviolet-ray clinics, UV treatment having been deemed as the most effective way to prevent rickets and other ailments. Children who, in the opinion of welfare clinic doctors, needed to convalesce were prescribed two months at the city's residential home. If a toddler had been a 'contact' of TB in the family home, he was taken to Carnbooth Home, in Carmunnock, where he stayed for between ten and twelve weeks.

For all the Corporation's efforts, there was one child-health area in which it was powerless – domestic accidents. Meg counselled, 'I can only urge that parents should take precautions against those so frequently fatal and completely avoidable accidents in the home, such as burns, falls and the eating by small children of poisonous pills and other medicines.'

Classrooms had improved by 1957 as well. Gone were the dingy pre-war paintwork and draughty passages, to be replaced by vivid colours, floor-to-ceiling windows and better teaching methods. Truancy was in retreat, too. As an example, Meg pointed to a 'model school' – Merrylee Primary, in Ashmore Road – with its bright curtains and a dining room 'that could grace a first-class hotel'.

Special provision was being made across Glasgow for girl pupils and intensive courses aimed at those who wanted to leave at the end of their fourth year to begin a commercial career were introduced. In 'residential flats' in the school, girls could learn how to cook, bake and sew and how to deal with labour-saving devices such as fridges and washing machines. Meg added, 'She will be taught how to budget for her 'family', how to entertain her friends, how to keep her home hygienically clean, how to choose attractive, tasteful furnishings.'

It was all, as the saying goes, a far cry from the very early days of the child-welfare campaign. James Burn Russell would surely have approved.

Graham Ritchie and Eleanor Alexander build up the 'bonnie' for Guy Fawkes Night. For many children, this night was the
highlight of the autumn. There were very few organised fireworks displays in the 1950s and most back tenements and gardens
had their own bonfires. 1951. Photographer: Unknown

'I've lost my mum!' A wee boy in Edinburgh, stranded on a city street, searches his pockets for some form of identification as a local policeman lends a sympathetic ear. The youngster, his knee scraped and bleeding, has his shoes on the wrong feet. May 1959.
Photographer: Duncan Dinsdale

'*Chariots of Fire* here we come!' The will to win shows on the faces of these boys at George Watson's College, Edinburgh, as they race towards the finishing-line in the final of the school's fifty yards under-six event. July 1957.
Photographer: Unknown

Not even the rain could dampen this young girl's fun on the beach at Brodick, Isle of Arran. She simply used her inflatable boat as a makeshift umbrella. Holidays abroad were practically unheard of in the 1950s and the West Coast of Scotland provided happy holiday memories for many children. July 1957.
Photographer: Frank Gray

Meet the Milky Bar Kids. Milk bars, such as this one in Maitland Street, Cowcaddens, Glasgow, caused much excitement when they were opened in the mid 1930s. Others cropped up in Anderston, Bridgeton, the Gorbals and Govan and they all promoted the health benefits of the white stuff to young, growing bodies. 1930s.
Photographer: Unknown

'Can't understand why we were left off the guest list, can you?' Left without an invitation to the ceremonies, these three youngsters stand waiting for a glimpse of Queen Elizabeth II during her visit to Glasgow. 1950s.
Photographer: Harry Moulson

Fishing on the dock of the bay. Youngsters gather on the pier at Rothesay, their eyes peeled for shoals of fish before dropping their lines and bait. Not a lot of thought was given to how you would get the fish back through the crack in the board if you landed the big one! 1956. Photographer: Unknown

'All aboard!' Sea Scouts from the 35th Company Thornlie Park cheer on their team-mates during a boat race against Renfrew Boys. The Sea Scouts, Guides, Brownies, Cubs and Scouts together formed a potent network offering discipline and healthy activities for countless thousands of Scots children. September 1951. Photographer: Harry Moyes

The Railway Children. Billowing clouds of smoke and steam envelop the railway platform at Barnton Station, Edinburgh. This was the very last train to leave Barnton for Princes Street Station, on 5 May 1951. The children who waved goodbye to the train weren't to know that the fabled era of steam had only slightly more than fifteen years' life left in it. Princes Street station itself has long since disappeared. Photographer: Unknown

No, the posters on this school wall had not been badly misspelt. They formed part of a phonetics lesson that kept these four kids utterly engrossed at Royston School, one day in Glasgow. 1965. Photographer: Jim Hamilton

Nine-year-old twins Audrey and Linda McDevitt look miserable despite their mum's consoling arm on their first day at Hunter Primary School, East Kilbride, in 1968. The family had just relocated from Shettleston. Thirty-six years later, Audrey admitted that Linda had quickly got over her trauma – but she herself came down with shingles and was off school for weeks.

Photographer: Allan Kean

The Fab One. Paul McCartney of The Beatles meets with the press in Edinburgh during the Fab Four's UK tour. The Beatles played in both Glasgow and Edinburgh at the height of their fame and the sound of their instruments was routinely drowned out by the volleys of screams from the fans. This was Beatlemania at its very height. October 1964.
Photographer: Unknown

ENTERTAINMENT

CHAPTER TWO

ENTERTAINMENT

On the night of Wednesday, 21 October 1964, in Glasgow, you could have gone to see Gregory Peck and Omar Sharif in *Behold a Pale Horse*, at La Scala, or watched Bernard Shaw's *Saint Joan*, at the Citizens. For some 6000 adolescents and teenagers, however, there was only one show in town – the Fabs were at the Odeon in Renfield Street.

At this stage in their career, The Beatles could do little wrong. Already that year they'd done two Ed Sullivan shows in the States (watched by more than 140 million viewers), had begun shooting their first film, *A Hard Day's Night*, and held the top six singles in an Australian chart, not to mention the first five in a *Billboard* chart.

Actually, the October show was the band's second in Glasgow during that barnstorming year. The first show was on 30 April and 6000 tickets had been snapped up in a frenzied postal ballot before they were even printed. The postal move had been designed to avoid a repetition of disturbances during queuing for tickets for The Beatles' Edinburgh shows, when the first fans had shown up on a Thursday, three days before the box office actually opened.

With their two performances at the ABC Cinema in Lothian Road over, the group came through to Glasgow for their Thursday-night concerts. They probably didn't have time to look at the Glasgow newspapers during their stopover. If they had, they might have been mildly amused by the *Glasgow Herald*'s leading article, titled 'Shriek!', about The Beatles phenomenon:

> Traffic may be brought to a standstill and the police be more sore-pressed than on cup-final day. After all, you cannot wallop a screaming 13-year-old over the head with a truncheon just because she seems intoxicated by the exuberance of her own vocabels.

So overwhelming was the reception that some 250 people, mostly young girls, had to be treated for shock or hysteria. Outside the Odeon, growling crowds of ticketless fans marched up and down nearby streets, kept on the move by the large police contingent. Touts were selling seventy-five sixpence tickets for twelve shillings each and souvenir programmes were going for at least two shillings over their two shillings and sixpence cover price.

Inside, if you were more than ten yards from the stage, you probably could not have heard the music, so deafening were the volleys of screams. By the time the first show was over, the cinema resembled, in the words of one nurse, a 'battlefield clearing station'.

As soon as the second show had finished, the band hurtled out of a side entrance into a waiting car, bound for Renfrew Airport, and were boarding their private plane within twenty-five minutes.

When the Fabs came back to Scotland six months later, global Beatlemania had, if anything, increased since that last week in April. 'The psychologists have tried to read all kinds of significance into their phenomenal success,' observed the *Evening Times*. 'Now a sociologist says they represent the duality of present-day society.'

As in April, the band played Edinburgh before arriving in Glasgow. The evening paper's 'Talk of the *Times*' columnist was plied with gin as he quizzed Paul McCartney. Paul refuted reports that the band paid a million a year in tax, saying, 'We don't pay as much as that. Mind you, we pay plenty,' he added, pulling out his empty pockets to prove it. He said that they'd been driving through the Stirlingshire village of Dumgoyne, eager for lemonade and cheddar cheese, and their road manager had had to foot the bill as the band was penniless.

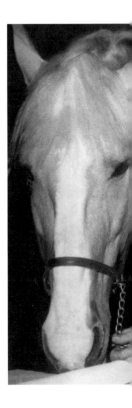

Disturbances were reported during and after the shows, with cars being overturned and shop windows being kicked in. Eight teenagers and a twenty-one-year-old man, arrested during disturbances, appeared at the Glasgow Central Police Court the following morning and the Lord Provost, Peter Meldrum, crossly laid into the 'hooligan element'.

Over the next couple of months, The Beatles would play their first concert in Liverpool in more than a year and the band would release their latest British LP, *Beatles for Sale*. During their final UK tour, in December 1965, they played Glasgow just one more time, shortly after receiving their MBEs from the Queen.

There was no Beatles-style adulation for Frank Sinatra when he arrived in Glasgow on Monday, 6 July 1953. He came to the city unobtrusively, by plane, and met only a small handful of fans as he strode into his city-centre hotel just after noon.

Sinatra's star had faded since his peak in the 1940s, when he had found fame and bobbysoxers' adulation both as a singer and as an actor. Indifferent film choices put paid to much of that, however. But Sinatra was Sinatra and his name was irresistible to a gaggle of journalists at the hotel who knew he would make good copy prior to his show at the Glasgow Empire. He chatted about his love of golf (he managed to fit in a visit to the Open at Carnoustie, where Ben Hogan won a memorable victory) and even about the then-current controversy over whether the BBC should have a commercial rival, specialising in what was called 'sponsored broadcasting'.

While not wishing to wade into the issue, Sinatra did say he admired much of the BBC's output, especially its televised dramas – and revealed that he'd like to know more about how these were done because he was thinking of ultimately working as a director or producer of TV programmes and films. He had watched commercial TV in the States and wondered how the scriptwriters managed to cope with the endless production conveyor belt.

As for his shorter-term future, he said he would do less and less singing and concentrate more on situation comedy.

The Renfield Street Odeon lasted longer than the Fabs did, closing down in January 2006.

'The pipe-in-hand Frank,' noted the *Evening Times* reporter, 'is a remarkably changed character from the chip-on-the-shoulder Frank we have read about. Glasgow should like him, more than somewhat.'

Within a year of that interview, however, Sinatra's star would be re-born thanks to his Oscar-winning role as Private Angelo Maggio in *From Here to Eternity*, opposite Burt Lancaster, Deborah Kerr and Montgomery Clift.

The Open Arms Hotel, at Dirleton, in East Lothian, had never seen anything like it. For none other than Brigitte Bardot, the glamorous French film star had unexpectedly shown up there.

Bardot was doing location shoots for her latest film, *Two Weeks in September*, posters for which would boast the memorable tagline, 'Suddenly... uncontrollably... Bardot in love as no woman ever loved before!'

Dressed in a green Shetland jumper and brown corduroy hipsters (this was the 1960s, after all), Bardot posed for photographers in the hotel garden, where a breakfast table of porridge, marmalade, rolls and coffee had been laid.

If La Bardot looked a trifle pre-occupied, it was because, as a spokesman let drop, her make-up, which had been specially flown in from France, had been held up in London.

Even on a golf course in Scotland, singer and actor Frank Sinatra could still look every inch the gilded film star. He's pictured here at the Open at Carnoustie, won by US golfing legend Ben Hogan, in what was Hogan's greatest ever year. July 1953. Photographer: Dunky Stewart

Sixties film goddess Brigitte Bardot heads off for a lunch break during the filming of *A Coeur Joie* (also known as *Two Weeks in September*), at Dirleton, East Lothian. The French girl was a pin-up for countless young men during the 1960s and 70s. BB, as she would become known, later became an animal rights campaigner. September 1966. Photographer: James Millar

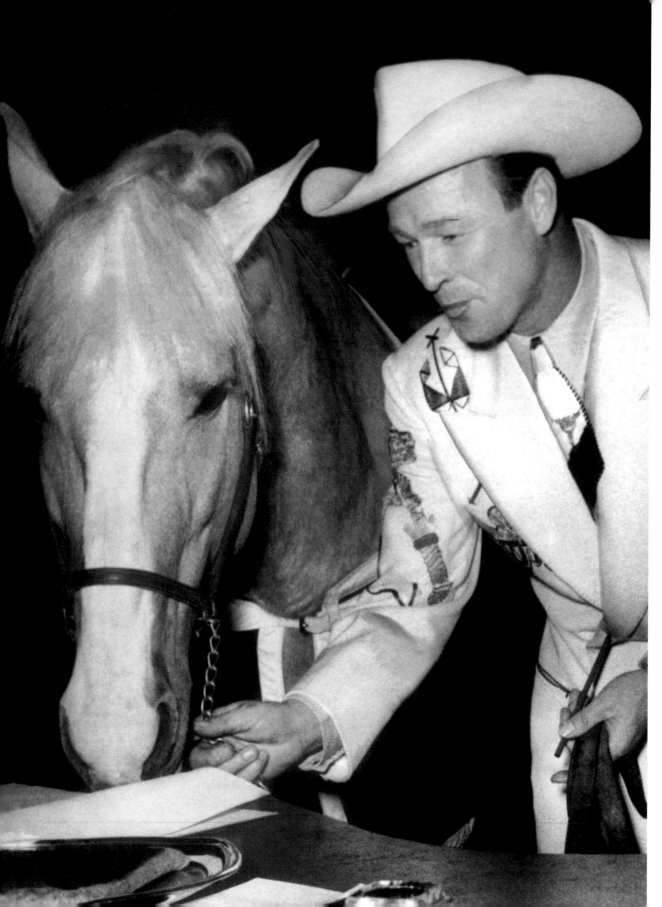

Country entertainer Roy Rogers and his famous horse, Trigger, signing the register at the Central Hotel, Glasgow, 1954. Thousands of delighted young fans turned up to meet the duo when they made a celebrity appearance in Glasgow. February 1954.
Photographer: Dunky Stewart

Rat-Pack star Sammy Davis
Junior looks supremely relaxed as
he jokes with photographers prior
to his one-night show in Glasgow.
Just three years earlier he'd
starred in the original *Ocean's
Eleven*. May 1963.
Photographer: Unknown

'Up persicope!' Spectators found these periscopes very handy when it came to trying to get a glimpse of the royals during a their visit to King's Park in Glasgow. 1937. Photographer: Dunky Stewart

THAT'S LIFE

CHAPTER THREE

THAT'S LIFE

Where would we be without our press photographers? It's not just that, without them, our picture library would look distinctly threadbare – it's that, time and again, as skilled fingers squeezed shutters, an offbeat or an unrepeatable moment is captured forever.

In this section, you'll come across lots of such moments. There's the woman, caught in an unexpected downpour without an umbrella, who tugs her overcoat over her head and strolls on unconcernedly, one summer's day in 1952. In a similar vein, twelve years later, there's a shot of spectators at a bowling match smiling through a downpour. Two men have hiked their jackets over their heads. Two women, more sensible perhaps, have their Rain Mates on. But it's the man in the middle, the one with the rueful grin and the cigarette in his mouth, who catches the eye. What's that on his head? Is it a Rain Mate? Surely not.

In one anthology of press photography, the following words appear:

A glance through the pictures is a reminder of photography's power to inform and communicate . . . Looked at carefully, much of the work presented here communicates with an emotional power and immediacy that words alone cannot achieve, sometimes presenting ideas and feelings that cannot be spoken. A carefully selected millisecond can summarise a lifetime's experience or symbolise a nation's progress.

The photographs that passage refers to had been shot in countries across the world but they can apply to the photographs included here and to the photographers who pressed the shutter.

For sheer drama, there's an arresting moment, glimpsed at Glasgow Airport in 1966, when journalists and spectators suddenly realise that a glider is about to land very close to where they are standing on the runway. Looking at the figures on the ground, especially the two in the centre of the picture, you can't help but feel their panic as they spot the inrushing glider. There's a distinct tension here – did the two figures make it to safety before the glider touched down?

There's another picture in this section of a lamp-lighter maintaining gas lights in Nicholson Street, in the Gorbals. Never mind that the tenements behind him have long been swept away – his own job disappeared with the last of the gas street-lamps, sometime in the early 1970s, apparently. But it's an evocative shot, with enough detail to make you want to look at the photograph for more than just a couple of seconds – the shattered windows and the graffiti on the wall and on the road. Then there's the man's satchel slung over the lamp.

What was in it? Did it contain his lunch? Or maybe the equipment he needed for his job?

Another long-gone occupation in these pages is that of the chimney sweep, once a familiar sight in smoky Glasgow. Here, one sweep, Alexander Matheson, tries to rescue a kitten named Tigger from a stack.

Elsewhere, there's the January 1957 fashion parade by art students. You can only imagine what the chap on the right, with the pipe, made of it all. Nearly two decades later, an underwear-clad model enjoyed being the centre of attention as she posed for passers-by. Is the man in the bunnet, who's obviously taken with her, in on the act somehow? Your eye is taken by the contrast between the model and the older woman to the right, in the heavy coat and zip-up boots. They both seem to be enjoying themselves, however.

The photographer's sharp eye is evident time and again here. It has spotted the man who has taken an impromptu nap – the worse for wear through drink, probably – in full view of people at a bus stop, who pretend they haven't noticed him. Then there is the female curler captured in action at Ayr ice rink – it's a great study of concentration and the cigarette makes it.

The great New York photographer Weegee (born Arthur Fellig) once recalled being told that his pictures of that city constituted a social document and deserved to be published in a book. 'To me,' he said, 'a photograph is a page from life and, that being the case, it must be real.' The photographers whose work has appeared, over the decades, in the *Evening Times*, the *Herald* and the now-defunct *Bulletin*, couldn't agree more.

'Mayday!' Pressmen and spectators dive for cover as an Air Training Corps glider takes an unconventional approach to the runway at Abbotsinch in 1960. The airstrip was used by the RAF and the Royal Navy before becoming Glasgow Airport in 1966.
Photographer: Unknown

A nice Scottish summer day on the
bowling green is interrupted by – what
else? – a torrential downpour. At least
these spectators at the Scottish Bowling
Association Championships, at Queen's
Park Bowling Club, Glasgow, kept up a
cheery front in the midst of the rain.
August 1964. Photographer: Allan Kean

This particular curler, identified for posterity as Mrs T. Veitch, of Gatehouse-on-Fleet, lets fly with a well-placed shot in a competition at Ayr ice rink. It's a perfect study in concentration – and you can excuse the cigarette on the grounds that not much was known about the dangers of smoking, back in the 1950s and 1960s. November 1960. Photographer: Edward Jones

No, this woman hasn't lost her head – she's just been caught in an unexpected downpour without an umbrella to hand. This particular summer shower soaked thousands of Glaswegians heading home after a long day at the office or on the factory floor. July 1952. Photographer: Unknown

The life of a chimney sweep in the city could be quite gruelling and challenging, especially so for sixty-five-year-old 'sweep', Alexander Matheson, who was tasked with rescuing a kitten named Tigger from a chimney stack. September 1955. Photographer: Unknown

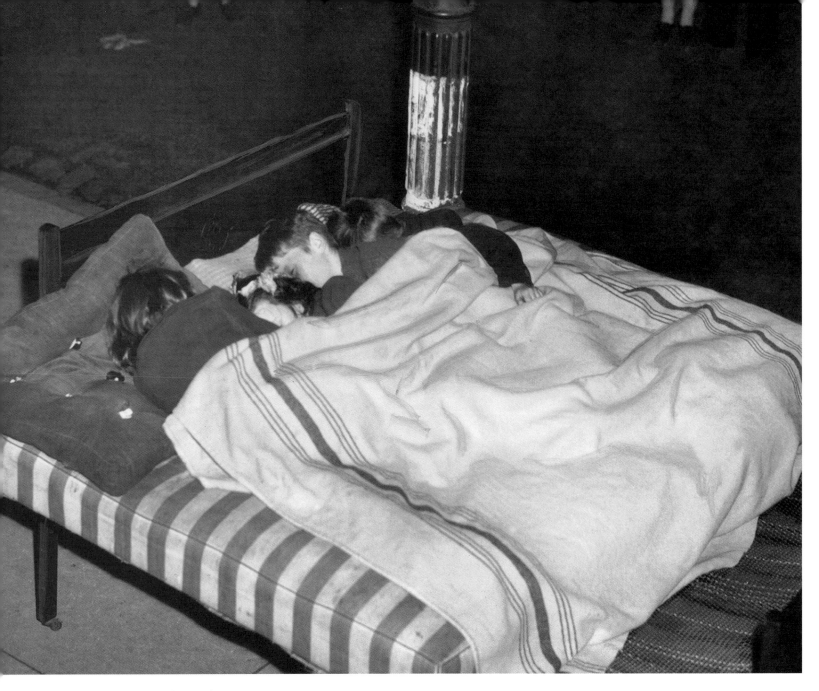

It was common for kids, in the immediate post-war years, to share a bedroom and even to share a bed but you can only speculate on the circumstances that might have led to these four youngsters sleeping together in this bed out on the street. 1956. Photographer: Unknown.

There are some days when the sheer hassle of Christmas shopping means you have to take the weight of your feet for a while and light up a cigarette, as this shopper, catching her breath in Glasgow's Argyle Street, did. The 'models' in the background regard her dispassionately. 1984. Photographer: Edward Jones

Waiting for a good Samaritan . . . or for the pubs to open? This Glaswegian has decided that there's little point to standing in the bus queue when he can take a nap, right there and then on the pavement. The people at the bus stop, in London Road, Glasgow, appear indifferent to his decision. 1970s.
Photographer: Unknown

Fashion Parade. Art students parade their latest designs through the streets of Glasgow much to the bewilderment of passers-by. January 1957. Photographer: Unknown

The hissing of the gas lamp was a sound to be heard throughout many city streets until 1971 when gas street lamps were finally phased out. This lamp-lighter, one of the city's small army of 'leeries', sets to work cleaning and maintaining the gas lights in Nicholson Street, Gorbals, Glasgow. 1960s.
Photographer: Unknown

A window of opportunity – this shop in Exchange Square, Glasgow, found a more unusual way of window dressing and catching the eye of passing shoppers – not to mention photographers! 1956. Photographer: Bert Paterson

Now here's something you don't see every day – the underwear-clad model in this fashion shoot in Glasgow enjoys being the centre of attention. She's watched by an amused crowd that includes several examples of an earlier trend in Glasgow fashion – woolly hat, thick wool coat and zip-up boots. 1975. Photographer: Unknown

The Central Hotel in Glasgow used to be the place where autograph-book-clutching fans could see all the showbiz stars who visited the city. Many famous faces were seen entering and leaving the famous hotel. Here, doorman Jimmy Cawley hails a taxi outside the ornate front entrance. 1957. Photographer: Frank Gray

Entertainer Ken Dodd takes time out from his role in *Startime* at Glasgow's Alhambra Theatre to hand out vaccine-impregnated sugar lumps to children at Bridgeton Child Welfare Clinic and Day Nursery. 'Doddy's' visit was part of a drive by Glasgow Corporation's Anti-Polio Campaign. April 1969. Photographer: Unknown

HEALTH

CHAPTER FOUR

HEALTH

On the day that the NHS was launched, Sir George Henderson, Scotland's health secretary, warned people against expecting too much of the service, too soon. He said the NHS would be developed gradually, by experiment and experience. His next words, however, reminded ordinary people why they had so looked forward to the NHS in the first place: 'The main substantial change . . . is that, from today onwards, all services can be free to the patient.' Free to the patient – people couldn't get used to the idea but they liked the sound of it. More than half a century on, it is difficult to imagine the furore – or the eagerness – that surrounded the creation of the NHS.

The need to do something meaningful to care for people from the cradle to the grave had been foreshadowed in 1942, in a radical report by Sir William Beveridge on social security provision. But the creation of the NHS attracted antagonism from the medical profession and from Conservative critics. However, the Tories came round to the idea once they realised that it was hugely popular with the electorate.

Eventually, on Monday, 5 July 1948, the NHS came into being ('New health service begins to-day', read the *Glasgow Herald* headline). Hospital and GP services had finally received the streamlining they badly needed. Overnight, the government gave itself the responsibility of promoting a comprehensive health service that aimed to improve the nation's physical and mental health.

In Scotland, some 80 per cent of GPs had enrolled with the service and more than 400 hospitals, with a combined total of some 65,000 beds, had passed into state ownership. Of the hospitals, 183 had been voluntarily run, 218 had been run by local authorities and seven had been in the control of the Department of Health for Scotland. In Glasgow, some 580 doctors had accepted service under the new Act. Only seventy were holdouts.

Scotland needed something like the NHS. As historian Tom Devine puts it, '[Its] problems of poverty, low incomes and poor health had always been more serious than the average for the UK as a whole and these historic reforms were likely to have a disproportionate effect for good on the welfare of her people.'

As Scotland's largest and most industrialised city, of course, Glasgow could be expected to benefit from the improved health services that were now on offer. According to historian Irene Maver, smallpox, diphtheria and measles were just some of the ailments treated by the half-dozen municipal 'fever' hospitals in the early decades of the twentieth century. Pollution and serious overcrowding resulted in more and more people contracting pulmonary tuberculosis. The

influenza outbreak of 1918–19 had killed some 4000 people. Throughout the inter-war period, infant mortality was an ever-present problem.

Pulmonary TB was a serious problem in the immediate post-war years. Some 2809 cases were notified in 1946 – far more than the average of 1650 for the five years between 1934 and 1939. Inadequate hospital accommodation and a shortage of nurses had caused a backlog of cases but health officers saw the figures as an argument for hastening the programme of slum clearance. On the bright side, the birth rate for 1946 – 25,391 – was the highest recorded in the last twenty years and the infant mortality rate was the lowest on record.

Public health issues aside, Scots surged in record numbers to register with the new NHS. The demand for drugs, dental and ophthalmic services, for dentures and glasses, was so heavy that the costs for the first year were forecast to be £8 million, £1.5 million more than the government had budgeted for. In July, more than 567,000 prescriptions were ordered – in Glasgow, in August alone, there were 177,000. The demand for dental treatment was said to have been 'extraordinary'.

'When we come to ophthalmics,' Sir William Marshall, a leading figure in the NHS in Scotland, noted dryly, 'so far as I can see, the whole population of Scotland is going blind. Glasgow to date has had 33,000 applications for spectacles, most of them for two pairs.'

The considerable success of the service across the UK was seized on enthusiastically by Aneurin Bevan, the combative Minister for Health. Speaking in mid September, he said that between 92 and 93 per cent of the entire population had now registered with their doctors. 'For myself, I am delighted,' he said, 'because it means that the NHS is a classless service. It means that every section of the community will begin to enjoy all its benefits and that any fear of taint will have been removed.' Taking aim at some of his critics in Fleet Street, he added:

> Of course, some newspapers have been full of jeers . . . about the rush for spectacles, although why editors should complain about giving people spectacles, I do not know. The only misgiving I have is that practically everyone will be able to read some of the nonsense they write.

There were two good reasons for the rush for NHS facilities, Bevan said. 'One is because we are all of us delighted to get what we want for nothing. The other is that a very large number of people needed what they could now get but what they could not afford previously.'

Ten years after the momentous inception of the NHS, the newspapers were eager to see what had changed. 'In 1958,' began the survey in the *Glasgow Herald*, 'the Scots are a more heavily doctored nation than in 1948. In case of serious illness, they stand a better chance of getting a hospital bed and of riding there in an ambulance'. Across the UK, there were more staffed beds – 12 per cent more than in 1948 – and ambulances had carried 8,400,000 patients and covered 84 million miles in the process. Scotland also had the only new general hospital to be built in

Britain in the past twenty years – the 156-bed hospital at Vale of Leven.

Further improvements were observed. Infant mortality in Glasgow was at 36 per 1000 live births in 1955, down from 77 per 1000 in 1947. In response to the still-high death rates from pulmonary TB, an innovative mass X-ray public health campaign was launched in the city in 1957. Irene Maver writes that some 715,000 people were screened in mobile units and almost 2000 active cases were detected as a result,

In the decades since, Glasgow has continued to make considerable strides in public health. The 'sick man of Europe' tag is still with us – high-risk lifestyles, drug abuse and continuing poverty have seen to that – but the situation is far better than it would have been without the intervention of the radical scheme that came into being one Monday morning in July 1948.

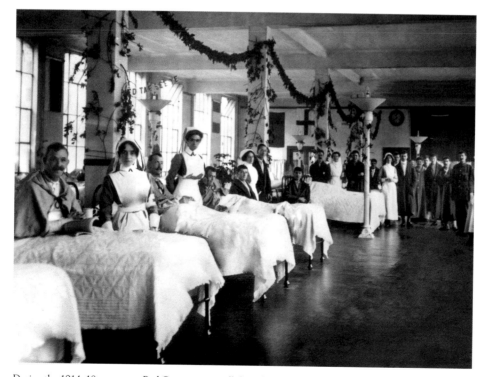

During the 1914–18 war, many Red Cross nurses staffed auxiliary hospitals, such as this one in Glasgow. The women were members of the local Voluntary Aid Detachment (VAD) and were trained in first-aid and home nursing. The men they looked after were generally the less seriously wounded and those in need of convalescence.

Photographer: Unknown

Nine-year-old Glaswegian George Davidson has to grin and bear it as he gets his teeth checked by Miss Elsie Webster. Free dental care had been introduced by the Labour Government in 1948 as part of the birth of the NHS – but by 1951 the service was so over-budget that charges were introduced for some dental care, such as false teeth, sparking a political row. March 1950.

Photographer: Unknown

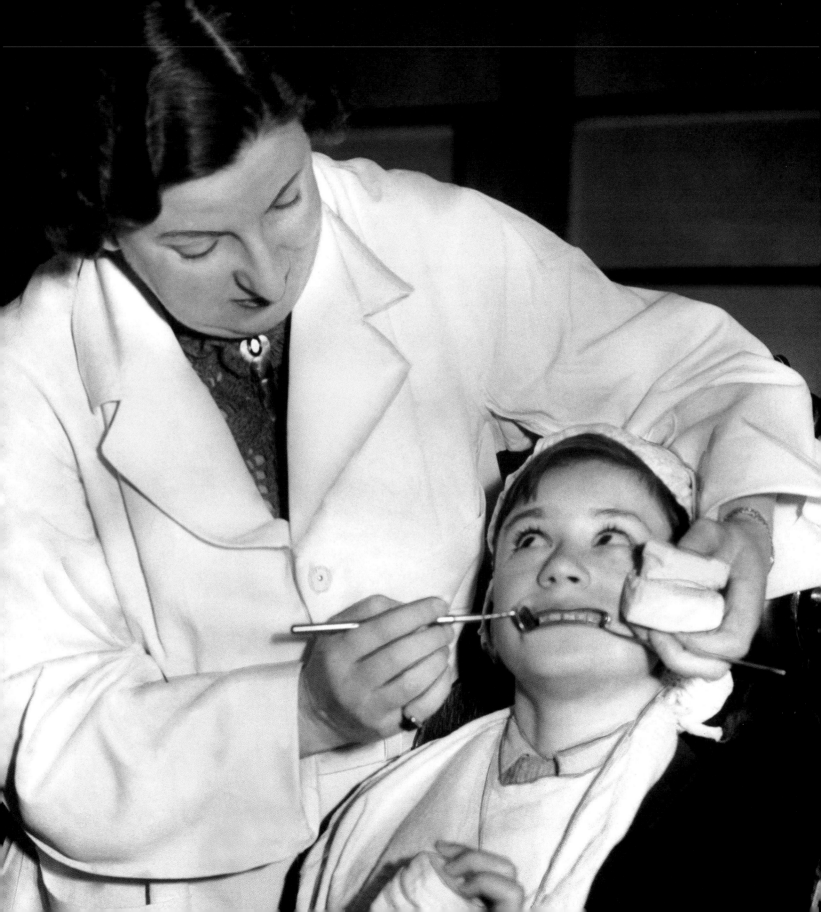

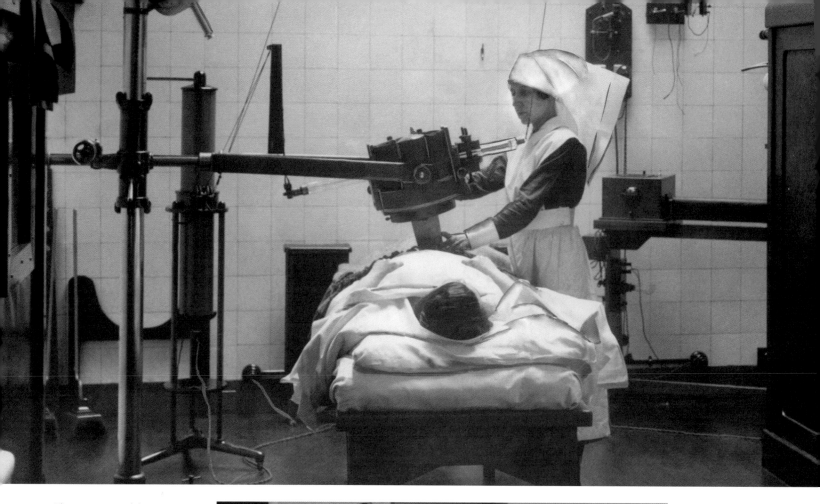

This was a state-of-the-art
medical facility eighty years ago.
The therapy at the Deep
Therapy Room at Glasgow
Royal Cancer Hospital included
the Enlangen treatment, seen
here – a form of X-ray imaging
that was said to be 'the most
advanced type of apparatus'.
February 1926.
Photographer: Unknown

Best foot forward –
children at Edinburgh's
Sighthill health centre
are given exercises by
physiotherapist Mr W.
Saunders to help prevent
them from developing
flat feet. January 1955.
Photographer:
Jimmy Thomson

Joan and Joyce Carr, twenty-year-old twin sisters and nurses, at Glasgow's Victoria Infirmary, measure out a patient's medicine. The photograph shows the extent to which nurses' uniforms have changed over the years – particularly the hats! June 1970. Photographer Harry Moyes

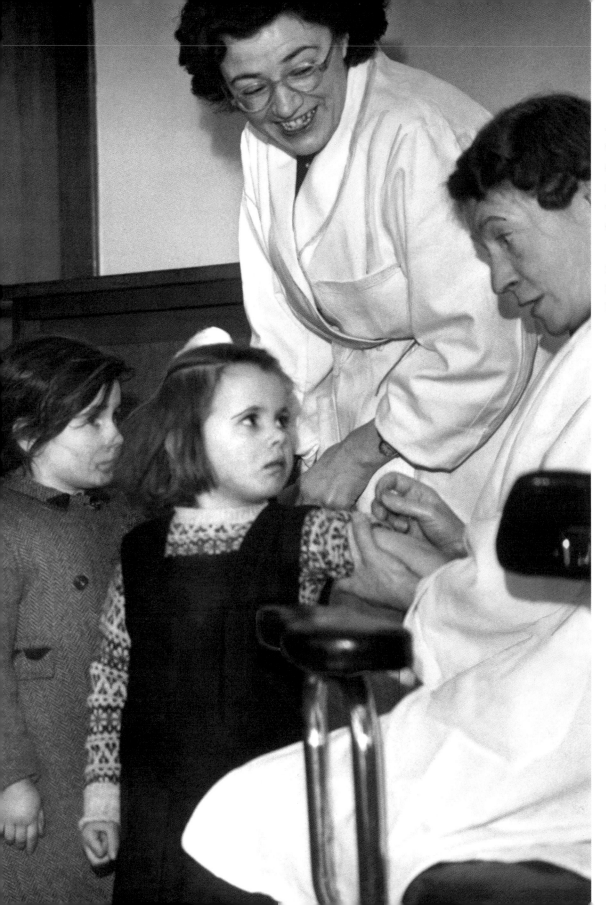

A look of apprehension crosses the faces of these children, photographed during an outbreak of smallpox as they wait for their smallpox vaccinations at Florence Street Clinic, Glasgow. Back in the early 1900s, the condition had often been present in the city in near-epidemic proportions. April 1950.
Photographer: Unknown

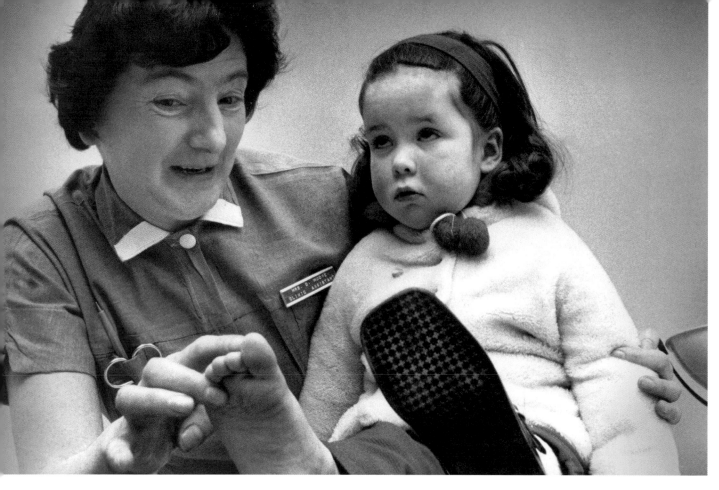

Yorkhill Hospital clinical assistant Mrs Doreen Moore checks that wee Joan Nicholson has all her piggies. March 1971. Photographer: Unknown

'Help, there's two of them!' A reluctant baby gets his nappy changed by student nurses in a mothercraft class, part of the nursery training on offer at Johnstone College. 1950. Photographer: Unknown

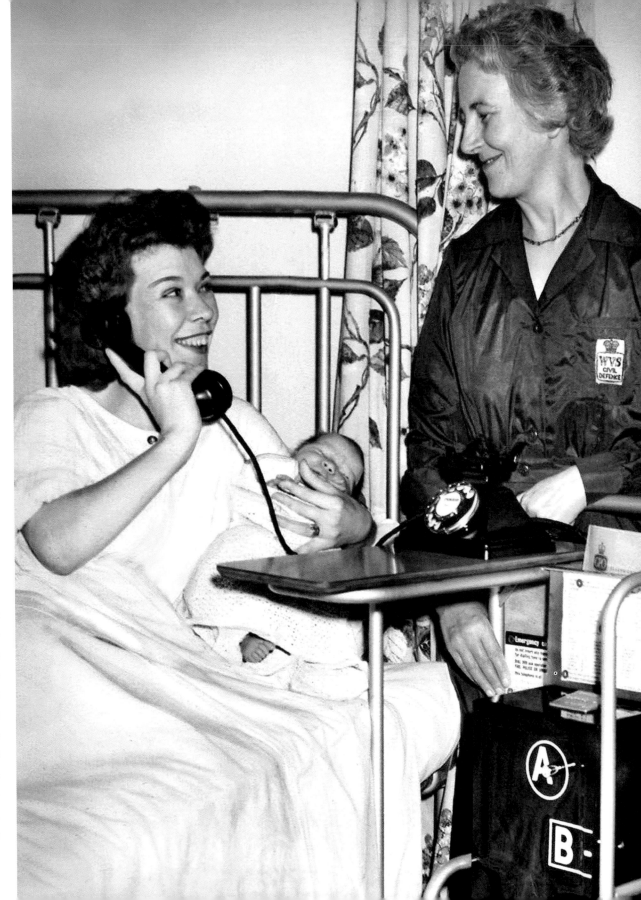

'Hello, darling, is that you?' The latest in mobile phone technology, the pay-as-you-go trolley phone, is used by mum Elizabeth Murrie as she cradles her four-day-old son, Paul, at Stobhill Hospital. Looking on is Mrs A. Swan, of the Women's Voluntary Service. The WVS raised the funds for the phone by selling items in the out-patients' canteen. July 1962. Photographer: Jim Hamilton

Looking down on the old St Enoch Square and the rail station. The station was opened in 1876 and eventually closed in 1966. It was later demolished in 1977 to make way for the popular St Enoch shopping centre. 1966.
Photographer: Dunky Stewart

that it is much older – or even that it is somewhere other than Glasgow. Few of the tenem[...]
pictured here survived.

The aerial shot of the Queen's Dock was taken in 1959, at a time when the Clyde still [...]
shipbuilding industry to speak of. How many of the workers in this part of the river could h[...]
foreseen that, within just twenty-six years, the dock would have been filled in to make way [...]
major concert and exhibition centre that would be used by millions of people? A £62 milli[...]
purpose-built arena, designed by Foster and Partners, is to be erected here as well, the first [...]
an ambitious £350-million development called QD2.

In contrast to the Queen's Dock picture, little appears to have changed since in the bus[...]
of Glasgow city centre, taken just one year earlier. But a closer look reveals subtle changes [...]
around George Square, the civic heart of the city.

The changes wrought at Ibrox and Celtic Park, however, have been anything but subtle[...]
Ibrox, pictured in 1959, was under the control of Scot Symon, who had taken over from Bi[...]
Struth five years earlier. Symon steered Rangers to six league titles, five Scottish Cups and [...]
League Cups, not to mention two European Cup Winners' Cup finals. In 1963/64, the club [...]
its second domestic treble. In 1959, Ibrox was then as much a fortress as it is now but the [...]
of January 1971, in which sixty-six fans died, prompted a far-reaching rebuild.

Like Ibrox, the Celtic Park of that era had large banks of uncovered terracing, which m[...]
have made for a pleasant afternoon in the depths of winter. Jimmy McGrory was in charge [...]
time this photograph was taken. The club had won the Scottish Cup in 1951 and 1954, th[...]
Coronation Cup in 1953, the league in 1954 and the League Cup in 1956 and 1957. Ahea[...]
the club, though, lay the managerial reign of the indomitable Jock Stein and, beyond him, [...]
McCann, who gave Celtic a stadium to be proud of.

What is evident is that both grounds have come to dominate their respective surroundi[...]
comprehensively as the clubs have come to dominate Scottish football.

When we're on a plane flying into Glasgow Airport and the weather conditions are goo[...]
get a vertiginous view of the city that never ceases to astonish. These archive aerial picture[...]
a similar view into the past.

AERIAL

CHAPTER FIVE

AERIAL

In his book, *Scotland from the Air*, photographer Jason Hawkes wrote that, to get a cohe
of Scotland, you needed to look at the bigger picture – at the social, industrial and cult
history of the country. Aerial photography, he ventured, could do the pictorial equivalen
'From the air,' he wrote, 'objects that are seen every day are metamorphosed into somet
and often quite unrecognisable but how they fit together becomes increasingly clear and
to contemplate.'

So it is with these pictures of Glasgow. Though none of them is new – that is, none
shows the city as it is today – they show Glasgow as it was at the time and are valuable
very reason. Everyday objects, seen from between 1500 and 2000 feet above, become so
new and, from today's viewpoint, sometimes unrecognisable.

The picture here of Glasgow in 1970, with no fewer than eight bridges fording the C
worth looking at in detail and not just because the river's ancient, unyielding course re
of that old adage of how the Clyde shaped Glasgow and Glasgow shaped the Clyde.

The city's character was in the process of change at the time. It had finally had to le
shipbuilding industry (the final hurrah, the launch of the *QE2*, had taken place three ye
earlier). Other traditional industries had, by and large, gone the same way. Great swathe
Victorian housing had been demolished by the city fathers in what the late Giles Gordor
referred to as 'a frenzy of social conscience (or something purporting to that)'. A new co
Glasgow was on the rise, as was, in time, a new identity as a cultural and shopping Mecc

The Kingston Bridge was the latest artery over the Clyde. The construction of this ar
M8 had not been without controversy. Anderston was never the same again and a giant
been driven through Charing Cross to make way for the M8, its victims including the G
Hotel and the Glasgow end of the Monkland Canal. But the road and the bridge at leas
effect of taking away much traffic from the city centre.

As can be seen from this 1970 picture, the demolition and the reconstruction still ha
way to go. In the future lay shimmering steel-and-glass office blocks, a succession of inte
hotels, the building of the SECC and the Armadillo on the in-filled Queen's Dock and t
emergence of a financial district on the old Broomielaw.

An equally arresting image is the one that shows the Cathedral, the Royal Infirmary a
surrounding areas taken in low light through a filter of haze. It is half a century old but it
unfamiliar, overcrowded contours, sweeping up to the horizon, might deceive you into th

The newly built Kingston Bridge
(top) adds another river crossing to
the Clyde. The bridge opened in
1970 and became very popular within
a short time. In one early twenty-
four-hour period, it recorded 37,074
vehicles. St Enoch station can be
seen on the right. 1970.
Photographer: James Millar

A stunning aerial picture, taken in low light, of Glasgow Cathedral, the Royal Infirmary and surrounding area. Late 1950s. Photographer: Unknown

The main line out of Central Station dominates this aerial picture of Glasgow city centre. Many of the old warehouses and tenements have long since disappeared, to be replaced by modern housing and office developments amid Glasgow's economic boom. 1960. Photographer: Dunky Stewart

The River Clyde looking down over Queen's Dock. The same area today houses the SECC, the Armadillo and the Moat House Hotel (now rebranded as the Crowne Plaza Glasgow). Note the ships and other vessels berthed along the Clyde. 1959. Photographer: Dunky Stewart

Rangers' Ibrox Stadium as it looked in 1959. The main façade of the stand still exists today but the rest of the stadium has seen major redevelopment in the wake of the Ibrox Disaster in January 1971. 1959.
Photographer: Unknown

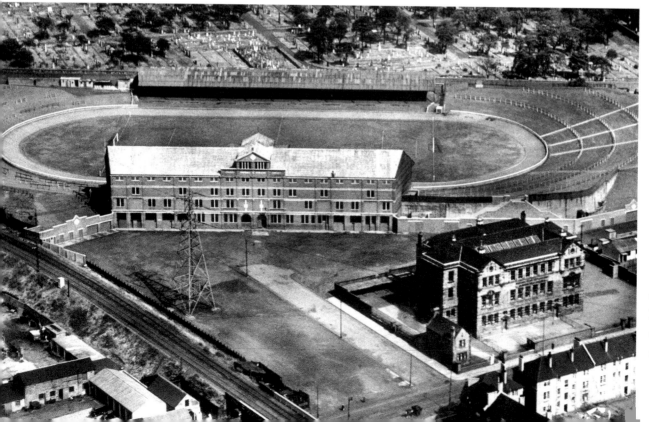

This is Celtic Park back in the 1950s during the era of Jimmy McGrory's reign as manager. London Road School, immediately to the front right of the ground, is still around although the stadium itself and much of its surrounding landscape have changed dramatically.
Photographer: Unknown

The famous grid layout of Glasgow city centre can be seen in this bird's-eye view of George Square and the surrounding area. Queen Street railway station can be seen centre left. Other landmarks, though, have gone. 1958. Photographer: Dunky Stewart

'Hold the front page!' Subeditors get to work on reporters' raw copy at the *Glasgow Herald* offices in Mitchell Street. The subs (as they are known), check the copy for mistakes and spelling and devise a headline to fit the story. March 1956. Photographer: Harry Moulson

NEWSPAPERS

CHAPTER SIX

NEWSPAPERS

In Michael Frayn's classic novel, *Towards the End of the Morning*, there's a lovely, evocative picture of Fleet Street as it used to be, in the mid 1960s. The editor is a 'short, rather fat man in a shapeless raincoat and a shapeless trilby hat', whose solitary form of communication with the world during office hours is to push typed notes to his secretary through a serving hatch.

To many of today's younger journalists, however, Frayn's view of The Street will come across as impossibly archaic. There's not a hint of new technology – no mobiles, no laptops – just gentlemen journalists at typewriters! They may have a point – print journalism has changed hugely over the last couple of decades, not just in the way in which news is collected but also in the way in which it's presented on the page. The digital revolution and the increasing influence of the internet will pose further questions for newspapers and the people who work on them.

But, to go back to the beginning, older reporters (those who will never see forty again, in other words) remember with crystal clarity the routine that would ensue when, together with a photographer, they were sent out to cover a breaking news story. They would speed to the scene, where they would identify and photograph witnesses or bystanders. With the clock ticking (deadlines were as unforgiving then as they are now), the photographer would hurtle back to the office to hand in the rolls of film, where they would be quickly developed in the darkroom and assessed by the picture editor.

The reporter, meanwhile, often had little choice but to sprint to the nearest phone box – usually, but not exclusively, a dank, draughty box on an isolated street corner – and, working from scribbled notes, would dictate the story over to a copytaker, sitting at the other end with a typewriter.

In the office, other reporters would type out their stories before subeditors – avuncular, patient souls, generally speaking – would scrutinise it for spelling and grammatical errors, and come up with headlines that told the story in a few succinct words.

Down in the composing room, the method of assembling type had remained virtually unchanged since the birth of the printing industry. Pressing inked metal on paper had been the basis of printing everywhere. Mechanisation gradually speeded the process but the principle remained unaltered. Compositors set the stories into molten lead type with Linotype machines (once memorably described as resembling 'a giant's typewriter with sound effects') while images of the photographs would be photo-engraved. Impressions would then be taken of the metal-cased pages. Each impression would be affixed by the machine men on to the drums of the huge rotary presses. At the press of a button, the presses would roar into life, churning out, at high speed, thousands upon thousands of copies of that day's paper.

Today, the situation could not be more different. Reporters on the spot use mobile phones to get their words back to the office from the scene in record time while the photographer sends the digital pictures to the picture desk by means of a WiFi-enabled laptop seconds after they have been taken.

In the office, reporters, their stories fortified by research done via e-mail or websites, typeset their own stories at their iMac screens. Sub-editors check it as before and devise headlines. Digital images of the photographs are dragged from an on-screen archive by means of a click of the mouse onto the on-screen page. Then the finished page is sent down the line to the printing plant, sometimes miles from the newsroom.

The revolution wrought in Fleet Street in the 1980s by Eddie Shah and Rupert Murdoch has been felt all across the country. Older hacks can be excused their occasional bouts of nostalgia – nostalgia for the distinctive smell of printer's ink mingled with sweat and cigarette smoke, the steady driving clatter of typewriters and the roar of the presses at edition time.

Veteran political journalist Chris Moncrieff summed it up when, lamenting the departure of Reuters' office in Fleet Street, he spoke of the old-style Street as being 'romantic and swashbuckling and splendid' and recalled a description of the place as being 'all drink and ink'.

But no one – not even Murdoch or Shah – could quite have foreseen the dramatic changes that would affect the print media. The new-technology revolution of the 1980s has become a digital revolution, with ordinary readers influencing content as never before. Now there are websites in which readers can decide on which stories get the most prominence. In a world in which speed is of the essence, it is not unknown for major stories to be broken by the authors of blogs and for their leads to be followed up by the print media.

The question of whether newspapers can survive in their present form has often been asked. It's a question that would have seemed utterly impossible just a couple of decades ago.

In an article of July 2006, *Guardian* commentator Victor Keegan looked at the complexities facing print journalism. He raised the question of what, if any, future, there is for newspapers 'as the creative destruction of the internet gathers pace'.

> The digital revolution is turning ordinary people into both creators of content (whether videos, online journals or books) and arbiters of the process that decides what gets published and how it is rated . . . now a new generation of news sites . . . which enable readers, not algorithms, to decide the prominence of stories is gathering force.

In Keegan's view, the survival of newspapers will depend on how quickly they absorb new technologies.

Newspapers may yet turn out to have a comparative advantage in becoming 'trusted sites' at a time when an explosion of blogs not only makes it impossible to read even the best of them regularly but also to decide what is true . . . [They] still have a vital role in generating trusted content. Whether it then appears on printed paper, on a portable screen, on a website complete with video (making it converge with television) or a mobile device . . . remains to be seen.

Trusted content? Websites? Blogs? Portable screens? You can only imagine what the gentlemen journalists who inhabit Frayn's novel would have made of such outlandish concepts.

In the machine-room foundry, sheets of papier mâché or 'flong' are placed into a mould. Molten metal is injected into the mould to produce metal printing plates known as stereotype. The plates were then clamped on to the press cylinders or rollers, ready for printing. 1930s. Photographer: Unknown

The news is on its way. Delivery vans wait for the first editions of the *Evening Times* outside the offices in Mitchell Street, Glasgow. 1930s.

Photographer: Unknown

The busy wire-room at the offices of the *Glasgow Herald* and *Evening Times*, in Mitchell Street. The teleprinter machines churn out incoming stories for the newspapers on streams of punched tape. The tape is then fed through a special reader which converts the coded message back into text. February 1936. Photographer: Unknown

Evening Times circulation staff use a portable printing machine, in the back of a van, to supply racegoers at the Lanark Races with the latest results from Liverpool and Bath. Newspapers and radio were the only sources of live information around this time. Today, it's a different story, with television, radio, the internet, fax, mobile phones and texting all able to relay news instantly. July 1938. Photographer: Hugh Dewar

An early version of today's paparazzi? Perhaps. Here, a group of photographers wait outside Glasgow Cathedral to get a shot of a society wedding. The photographers are using a variety of different camera formats from VN glass plate models to 35mm film. 1940s. Photographer: Dunky Stewart

Capturing King George VI on camera in the process department of the *Glasgow Herald* and *Evening Times*. Pages were photographed in the process department to make negatives as part of the page-printing process. 1940s. Photographer: Unknown

Operators at banks of Linotype machines (automated typesetters) compose lines of type or 'slugs' which are then made up into pages. For decades, typesetting was done by hand – a painstaking process! 1940s. Photographer: Unknown

Printers check copies fresh off the press in the printing hall of the *Glasgow Herald* at Mitchell Street. October 1968. Photographer: Jim Hamilton

This is how pages in the *Evening Times* and *Glasgow Herald* used to be made, in the days before new technology. Compositors would carefully assemble each page in the caseroom. Once the typeset pages were complete, a papier mâché impression would be made. November 1968. Photographer: James Millar

'Children adore me,' said
screen siren Mae West
when she first arrived in
Glasgow. So it proved.
This young Glasgow fan was
certainly taken with
Mae, who was known for her
colourful films and
sense of humour. All of
Glasgow, in fact, lay at
Mae's feet. November 1947.
Photographer: Unknown

MORE ENTERTAINMENT

CHAPTER SEVEN

MORE ENTERTAINMENT

An intriguing chain of events was set in motion by one of the photographs in this section.

Hollywood star Gene Kelly was pictured in Glasgow in 1953 but, beyond a few sketchy details (such as the fact that he hadn't long made *Singin' in the Rain*, which in time would become a classic), we could not work out why he had visited the city half a century ago. The reasons, it was said, were 'lost in the mists of time'. Then an e-mail arrived from California and, at a stroke, cleared the mists and put us in the right direction. 'He was actually in Scotland,' it said, 'with the producer Arthur Freed, scouting locations for the film of *Brigadoon*. Regrettably, the studio eventually decided not to make the picture in Scotland and, to Gene's chagrin, opted for the backlot of MGM instead.' *Brigadoon*, which was released in 1954, tells the story of a mystical village in Scotland that comes to life for only one day every hundred years.

The e-mail was from Gene's forty-seven-year-old widow, Patricia, who had been alerted to the photograph in the first place by a Google alert on her home computer. Our interest piqued, we e-mailed Patricia back and then phoned her. During one phone call, we heard ourselves asking Patricia if she would consider flying all the way from LA to Glasgow to speak about her late husband's career. It was an invitation made on the spur of the moment. We thought that she might be too busy to come here and, after all, it was a long way. Nevertheless, she agreed.

So it was, on two nights in late January 2006, that Patricia, showing no visible signs of jet lag, entertained two full-house crowds at Glasgow's Mitchell Library, in the same hall where the photograph of Gene took pride of place amid the others in the *Picture This* exhibition. She is proud of that photograph and rightly so – even in a flat cap and tweed overcoat, there was no mistaking the debonair figure of the man who was one of Hollywood's finest dance stars.

Gene and Arthur Freed spent two days in Scotland in April 1953, arriving in Glasgow from London. While in Glasgow, Gene took in the Celtic Ballet at the Theatre Royal and, in the company of Arthur, he toured Burns country, Ayrshire, and Edinburgh. The photograph was taken when the actor was walking down Glasgow's Gordon Street. Nobody gave him a second glance – it was only when he smiled the Gene Kelly smile that passers-by recognised him. Two girls shook his hand and, elated, ran to tell their friends. Within moments, a crowd had gathered, complete, inevitably, with a press photographer.

'Gene really wanted to do *Brigadoon* in Scotland,' said Patricia, 'because he had such a vision of all the clans coming over the hills to the sound of bagpipes, like a John Ford western. I think it would have been magnificent.'

Gene first met Patricia in 1985. They were married five years later and were together until Gene's death in February 1996, at the age of eighty-three.

It was a Friday in the middle of July and there was a war on. The year was 1941 – a decisive one in the course of the war, as it turned out. At the start of the year, with Hitler engaged in one strategic plan after another, Churchill had a succession of meetings in London and in Scotland with Harry Hopkins, President Roosevelt's personal emissary. Churchill was hugely relieved by Hopkins' assurances that Roosevelt would supply Britain 'with the means of survival and of victory'. But, within a few months, Winston grew alarmed by the huge losses of ships and cargoes in the Atlantic. The situation grew so bad that he was convinced that only vast tons of shipping from America would allow Britain to pull through.

On Friday, 19 July, Hopkins made what the newspapers described as 'statements of far-reaching significance' at the US Embassy in London. America, he said, would build vast numbers of merchant ships, airplanes and tanks to help in the effort against the Germans. 'US supplies for Britain to whip Hitler' read the headline in the *Glasgow Herald*.

Just beneath this report was another, of a more anodyne sort – but one which reminded readers of the official campaign to boost morale in the Home Front

Shortly after noon, an ENSA van pulled up outside a Clydeside shipyard. Its occupants spilled out and, within minutes, had erected a tiny stage, complete with loudspeakers. A pianist and a small band busied themselves with a quick rehearsal. Shipyard workers climbed the scaffolding to get a better view of the stage. Others watched from the newly laid keels of ships. Then a roar went up as Gracie Fields – comedienne, film actress and music-hall star – took to the stage on the first Clydeside concert of her tour of Scotland's industrial heartland.

The workers, observed the *Herald*, 'formed a mass of brown and blue in the grey light . . . The scene that greeted [her] eyes as she stepped onto the tiny platform was probably unique in her experience.'

After twenty minutes of songs and recitations, Gracie smiled, waved and disappeared, leaving her audience, in good showbiz tradition, eager for more. The happy crowd surged around her car and a large group of cheering children stood at the gates to bid farewell.

America might just have agreed to give Britain more merchant shipping but the news probably took second place that day to the presence of an effervescent singer called Gracie.

If you thought that today's showbiz correspondents could be bitchy, you should have read Sheila Watson, a writer on the *Glasgow Herald*. In November 1947, having been assigned to meet Mae West in a London hotel prior to an appearance in Glasgow in the play, *Diamond Lil*, Ms Watson told readers that she had previously met ten 'glamour girls' in the same hotel.

To my dim female eye, the average pin-up looks poisonous. Not to put too fine a point on it, there are times when I feel like drowning the lot, with the exception of Rita Hayworth . . . Drowning her would be wasteful, but she should be made to swim for life; a photogenic face can be fatal. Now Miss West is untroubled by any such handicap . . .

Not a good start, then, but Mae charmed Watson, who noted her 'wide, handsome mouth, with a sunny smile', the rest of her appearance deriving from 'cosmetics, eyelashes, jewellery and the right gown'.

Mae, the larger-than-life star of stage and screen, had a certain reputation for lasciviousness but she impressed the *Glasgow Herald* writer as being 'a real humorist – vital, calm, cheerful, and with all the resources of fifty footlit years behind her.'

Watson's verdict on Mae? 'I deplore glamour girls but would spare Rita – and – yes, Mae.'

A week later, the star turned up at Glasgow's Alhambra and stole the show with what one critic described as 'the husky voice, the blonde hair, the famous figure – and the shimmy.'

A long line of Hollywood stars have made their way to Scotland over the decades, drawn, if not by the weather, then by the wide range of outdoor activities, from golf and fishing to shooting and hillwalking.

Jimmy Stewart was one such star. In October 1959, on holiday in Stonehaven, he treated himself to a day's shooting in the moors of Kincardineshire. The blustery weather didn't stop Jimmy from enjoying himself. Clutching a pheasant that had fallen to gun, he said, 'We bagged three or four but I must confess we saw plenty which are still flying.'

Pin-up British actor Dirk Bogarde takes a break from filming *Hunted* in Portpatrick, Dumfries and Galloway. The film, which was directed by Charles Crichton (who would later make *A Fish Called Wanda*) featured Bogarde as a man on the run after committing a crime of passion. August 1951. Photographer: Unknown

Screen beauty Jean Simmons, then just twenty, chats with Mrs Joseph McLachlan as they admire the table lamp she had presented to Mr McLachlan for being the 300,000 visitor to the Kelvin Hall. Just the previous year, Jean had earned an Oscar nomination for Best Supporting Actress in the role of Ophelia opposite Laurence Olivier in *Hamlet*. September 1949. Photographer: Unknown

Liz Taylor looking like a million dollars as usual. The screen beauty, photographed in Glasgow, had shot to fame in 1944 in *National Velvet*. Here she is wearing an expensive dyed moleskin coat. She sometimes carried a transparent plastic handbag, of which she said, 'I like it very much, because you can wear it with anything.' June 1951. Photographer: Bill Amos

Jimmy 'Snozzle' Durante, pictured here having breakfast at the Central Hotel in Glasgow, found fame as a comedian, composer, actor and singer – but it was his large nose that gave him much of his fame and fortune! July 1956. Photographer: Dunky Stewart

It's a wonderful life. Hollywood star James Stewart holds aloft one of the pheasants which fell to his gun during a shoot in Kincardineshire. It wasn't just on the set of Hollywood westerns that Jimmy handled firearms! October 1959. Photographer: Unknown

A great catch! Little Allan Peters proudly shows Scots-born film star Gordon Jackson a goldfish that he had won on the stalls at Paisley Unionist Fete. Not surprisingly, Allan was moved to name his new pet Gordon. Mr Jackson looks suitably grateful! July 1950. Photographer: Harry Moyes

'Sing as we go . . .' Gracie Fields sings to a huge audience of Clydeside shipyard workers. 'Our Gracie', as she was affectionately known, was a comedienne and a music-hall singer, who also appeared in a number of films. Fittingly, she had recently made a film called *Shipyard Sally* when she visited the Clyde. July 1941. Photographer: Dunky Stewart

Gene Kelly hadn't long added the 1952 smash hit, *Singin' in the Rain*, to his CV when he arrived in Glasgow. Perhaps another soon-to-be-made film was more appropriate to this picture – *It's Always Fair Weather*. Gene is pictured outside Central Station. April 1953. Photographer: Dunky Stewart

Even in the thick fog in George Square, there's no mistaking the lofty outline of Sir Walter Scott's column. Closer to the camera is the statue of William Ewart Gladstone, the illustrious politician who dominated British politics for much of the nineteenth century. December 1957. Photographer: Edward Jones

THE FOG

CHAPTER EIGHT

THE FOG

Fog, as can be seen from the photographs here, can add a moody element to the most everyday of scenes. A shot of three people crossing a footbridge which, on a sunny day, wouldn't merit a second glance, on a foggy day, resembles something from a 1940s film noir.

But, when fog met smoke, it meant smog – a word apparently coined in Glasgow – and the result was anything but pleasing. Glasgow, in common with other large, industrial cities, suffered badly from smog in the long decades before smokeless fuels and smoke-free zones became the norm. But nowhere, in the UK at least, suffered to quite the same extent as London. For five days in December 1952, the UK's capital was choked by a poisonous darkness. Many died at the time, others succumbed in the months and years afterwards – some 12,000 in all, according to one authoritative claim a few years ago. A London medical report of the time records, 'By the time the fog had lain over London for two days and three nights, the death rate had risen to a height last experienced in the city in the influenza epidemic of 1918.'

In late November and early December of that year, fog descended on Glasgow, though the casualty toll was nowhere near as serious as London's. The city was lucky enough to escape with a few minor incidents – bus drivers abandoning their vehicles between Blantyre and Cambuslang, a Rothesay–Gourock steamer getting stuck for three hours and a Glasgow drunk mistaking two women in a foggy street for his wife and daughter and assaulting one of them.

Smog wasn't exactly a new problem. For a century, Glasgow had been trying to address the issue of smoke abatement – none too successfully, if newspaper reports of the time are to be believed. In 1909, some 1000 people died in the thick, inescapable industrial fog. But at least there were signs in 1952 that the city was alert to the dangers of smoke pollution. The city's air-quality analyst, Magnus Herd, said the pollution did not stem from belching smokestacks, as many believed, but was mainly caused by domestic fires. Tests had shown that, on Sundays, when most factory furnaces were shut, the amount of pollution dropped only slightly compared to the rest of the week.

At the same time, the city's medical officer of health, Dr Stuart Laidlaw, warned that atmospheric pollution might be linked to cancer and said that exhaust fumes and cigarette smoke had to be looked at in light of the rapid increase in lung cancer over the past twenty-five years.

In December 1952, after a weekend of what it described as a 'pestilential murk', the *Glasgow Herald* called on Glasgow people to copy Manchester and Coventry by pressing for the setting-up of smokeless zones, until the National Coal Board could get round to providing everyone with

smokeless fuel. Ten months later, when the National Smoke Abatement Society brought its annual conference to Glasgow, the newspaper greeted them with the words:

> A steady look at the filthy, begrimed masonry of our buildings and a breathing for three days of our polluted atmosphere – even if rain-washed for the occasion – ought to send delegates away with renewed determination to carry on their good work of attacking the public conscience. For in essence these conditions are with us only because people put up with them.

Glasgow's Lord Provost, Thomas Kerr, told the conference it was high time that smoking was banned in cinemas, theatres and other public places.

The *Herald* might have worried that, as far as smoke pollution went, it was banging its head against a brick wall – particularly a filthy, begrimed one – but plans were being put forward for smokeless zones in various parts of the country, central Glasgow among them. Plus, a high-powered committee, under Sir Hugh Beaver, was already lining up a detailed look at air pollution. It visited the central Glasgow zone in April 1954. When the committee reported that November, it proposed a handful of measures, including a Clean Air Act, with the aim of reducing smoke in industrial and residential areas by four-fifths in ten to fifteen years.

Air pollution, said Beaver, cost Britain £250 million a year, to say nothing of a yearly wastage of around ten million tons of coal. In Clydeside, he added, the death rate from bronchitis was 'commonly much higher than in the rest of Scotland'. In 1952, 11.7 per cent of male deaths and 9 per cent of all female deaths had been due to respiratory disease. Across the rest of Scotland, the figures were 7.5 and 5.6. Among his measures were smoke-control areas in which the use of bituminous coal in houses would be restricted and cash aid provided for home-owners to pay for the conversion of appliances in control areas.

Glasgow and Edinburgh were planning smokeless zones and Sir Patrick Dollan, a former Lord Provost of Glasgow, said this trend should be encouraged. For a start, he said, it would boost the country's tourist trade.

> Glaswegians need only think of how lovely the atmosphere is over Clydeside during the annual Fair holiday to appreciate what their city could be made all the year round if smoke is combated with energy and speed in the same way as any other social disease is fought.

Nevertheless, smog continued to pose a health threat. In the first six months of 1959, more than 700 people died from bronchitis – some 400 more than the average yearly figure.

It wasn't until later that year – at the stroke of midnight on Wednesday, 14 October – that a smoke control area was established over 201 acres of central Glasgow. The area contained 367 houses and 380 commercial and industrial premises and the Corporation saw this as just the first step in a plan which, over the next five years, would help reduce Glasgow smog. Housewives would not have to spend so much of their time cleaning sooty furnishings. Businesses would see less decay in their buildings and fewer goods being spoiled. Industrialists would see less expensive fuel wastefully going up in smoke. Glaswegians, in time, would be able to breathe more easily again.

The story might have ended there but, as everyone knows, pollution is still around in 2006. Could someone get around to banning cars?

A Glasgow tramcar noses its way through the fog towards the camera. You might think that this picture was taken sometime in the evening but, in fact, it was taken at 2.45 p.m. February 1954. Photographer: Unknown

In a scene reminiscent of an atmospheric, pre-war, black-and-white movie, passengers wait for the Finnieston Ferry to berth amid thick afternoon fog on the Clyde. February 1954. Photographer: John MacKay

Selling the *Evening Citizen* newspaper in the early evening fog in Glasgow in the 1950s. The *Citizen* was a Glasgow evening paper which closed down in 1974.
Photographer: Unknown

Pigeons scatter into the freezing fog at the approach of a passer-by in Princes Street Gardens in Edinburgh – though others are content to stay where they are. And is that a pigeon on the man's right shoulder? December 1969. Photographer: Duncan Dinsdale

Passers-by crossing the fog-draped
South Portland Street suspension
bridge in Glasgow. This was taken
at 2 p.m. one winter's afternoon.
December 1951.
Photographer Harry Moyes

'Wish my bus would come – I'm freezing here!' Would-be passengers wait at a city centre bus stop, peering through the fog for a sign – any sign – of the bus that would take them home. January 1959. Photographer: Frank Gray

A murky night in Glasgow at the junction of Renfield Street and Argyle Street. Note the presence of the Cable Shoes store – a familiar landmark for visitors to the city centre for years. February 1959. Photographer: Unknown

'Don't interrupt me now, I'm just coming to my favourite bit!' Four-year-old Jean Aitken is captivated by her copy of *The Dandy* comic as she waits at Waverley Station for her holiday train to Cowdenbeath. Children's comics, such as *The Beano*, *The Dandy*, *Topper* and *The Beezer*, were popular for decades and some are with us still. April 1954. Photographer: Unknown

ON THE MOVE

CHAPTER NINE

ON THE MOVE

The Glasgow Fair of July of 1953 was, in Glasgow terms, little different from that of many previous Julys. Like iron filings drawn towards a magnet, the population was lured towards the bus and rail stations and to Renfrew Airport, with suitcases and kids in tow.

An *Evening Times* reporter, mixing with the crowds at St Enoch Station, glanced at the orderly scenes around him, at the police officers and railway officials smoothly channelling the holiday-makers towards their platforms, and noted, 'All the fun of the Fair was evident – harassed mothers, laden fathers and excited, smiling and "greetin" children.' He added, 'Many families were only going on holiday for one week but they still took with them almost everything but the kitchen sink. Prams, bicycles, camp-beds, tents, kit-bags and a tremendous array of suitcases were piled high in the left-luggage department.'

The scene was repeated at Queen Street Station, at Central and at the bus stations but it was already evident that, compared with previous years, there was little of the 'carefree chaos' that usually marked a Glasgow Saturday in July. The days when policemen had to regulate the great queues around Central Station seemed to have vanished. 'In the streets of the city itself,' observed an *Evening Times* reporter on Saturday, 18 July, 'there was an air of almost Sunday quiet. Most shops and business premises were closed and few pedestrians were about in the streets.'

The most popular destinations in Scotland included Edinburgh, Dunfermline, Oban, Aberdeen, Inverness, Gourock and the Clyde Coast resorts. At the airport, at the peak of the Glasgow Fair, planes bound for Ireland, the Isle of Man and the south were taking off every ten minutes. In the suburbs, buses waited in side-streets, earmarked for sunny destinations or conducted tours.

But many – perhaps an increasing number – of holidaymakers were letting the train take the strain and heading across the border. Many went to London, while others settled for Blackpool, Southport, Manchester and Scarborough.

The previous summer, 1952, in comments that throw interesting light on the stirrings of the post-war boom in mass travel, the *Evening Times* had detected this southwards shift in the Fair holiday pattern.

British Rail, faced with dwindling revenue and fierce road competition, had yielded to the 'tremendous demand' for cheap, long-distance travel by introducing the seventy-shilling Starlight Special to London. It had been a great success even though it was hedged by eight- and fifteen-day restricted availability. 'Who can doubt,' asked the author of the paper's City and Clyde

column, 'that the pressure will now be redoubled for equally favourable rates – in comparison with the road services, that is – to other holiday destinations?'

Rail still faced competition not only from road services but also from air, which was beginning to eat away at 'first-class' holiday traffic. 'What [rail bosses] will do in a few years' time, when 100-seater aircraft operating at around 1d a mile may be possible, is anyone's guess.'

The Clyde Coast, he argued, would never be insolvent – not with its status as a seaside 'lung' for the urban masses of Glasgow and Lanarkshire:

> [B]ut every Starlight Special and Dakota [aeroplane] leaving Glasgow this weekend carried away at least some money that might have been spent in the Firth. Economic conditions at the moment . . . are all against any major development plans, but the plans ought to be on the drawing-board at least . . . the drift from the Clyde can be arrested if the coast towns will take the trouble to find out just what makes a modern resort tick.

You can only speculate about what he would have made of the situation today, when, each year, Glasgow Airport flies nearly nine million passengers via more than fifty airlines to almost eighty destinations across the globe. When it comes to it, what would he have made of the numbers of Scots – an estimated 70,000 every year – who are selling up and moving abroad for good? The Office of National Statistics found in 2005 that emigration had reached its highest-ever level in 2003, with 190,000 Brits quitting the UK for abroad.

An April 2005 survey found that nearly three-quarters of young Britons were considering moving abroad – though another survey, in August 2006, suggested that Scots were the least likely to want to live abroad. The trend in emigration has been affected by several factors – the growth of global backpacking, people moving abroad to work and the hankering of people of a certain age for retirement villas in sunny European countries.

Scottish emigration has traditionally been associated with the Highland Clearances (though some historians argue that the Lowland Clearances caused many more evictions) but a key episode was Australia's bold post-war campaign to 'Populate or Perish'. From 1947 onwards, an assisted passage scheme encouraged Britons to relocate to Australia for a subsidised fee of just £10 – 'the £10 Poms'. The only condition was that they had to stay Down Under for a minimum of two years or else repay the cost of their outwards fare.

Thousands of Scots responded over the decades. In fact, between 1947 and 1982, some 1.18 million Brits packed up and headed to Australia. Many families prospered. Others, homesick, or painfully aware that they had ageing parents back home who needed to be taken care of, returned home. For proof of how many Scots have re-settled abroad, not just in Australia but in dozens of other countries, you only have to look up the numbers of Caledonian, Scottish and St Andrew's societies there are – they are everywhere from Cape Cod and Cyprus to Dubai, Hawaii,

Hungary, Russia, Thailand and Japan. And many Scots have launched outstanding careers abroad, in business, academia and showbiz. From comedian Craig Ferguson, now hosting *The Late Late Show* on CBS in the States to John Paterson, a US-based vice-president at IBM, Scots have not been slow to make their mark beyond their native shores.

There is, of course, a downside to this migration. Politicians and industrialists have long fretted about the drain of skilled Scots abroad – the Scottish Council (Development and Industry) issued a warning about this as long ago as October 1952. It's the same story today. No wonder politicians are appealing for skilled migrants to come to Scotland and are urging expats to consider returning home, before emigration and other factors combine to bring Scotland's population beneath the five-million mark sooner rather than later.

'It'll be a long time before we see this again.' Youngsters Jeffrey and Helen Chandler with their suitcases (and doll) prior to boarding the S.S. *Cameronia* at Yorkhill Quay. Their destination? Sydney, Australia. September 1950. Photographer: George Ashton

War-time service personnel (in the foreground, in uniform) encounter huge crowds of civilians queuing in Union Street, Glasgow, waiting for the trains that would take them from Central Station to the coast and other holiday resorts. Note the lamp-post sign reading 'shelter' – the place where people would have hidden away during German air-raids. July 1943. Photographer: Dunky Stewart

A fantastic panoramic shot of queues outside St Enoch Station for the annual holiday exodus to the Ayrshire coast. The queue even reached Dixon Street. Both the station and the adjacent hotel had disappeared by the mid 1970s. July 1943. Photographer: Dunky Stewart

A family from Dumbarton – Mr and Mrs Douglas Dow and their children, May (13), Douglas (12), Colin (10), William (6) and Elizabeth (4) – wait to board a flight from Prestwick to London, where they would catch a flight to Ontario, Canada. March 1951. Photographer: Harry Moyes

The fine art of forming an orderly queue reaches a new height in this scene at Port Dundas, with Glaswegians patiently waiting for buses that would take them down south for their summer holidays. Spotting where the queue begins and ends is difficult! July 1972. Photographer: Unknown

'Haste ye back!' A final farewell for Scots families bound for a new life in New Zealand, as they board the *Captain Cook* at Plantation Quay, Glasgow. Did any of them ever return? October 1956. Photographer: Frank Gray

'Next, please!' During the 1950s, countless Scottish families took the opportunity to emigrate to Canada. In order to process their applications, they frequently joined long queues, such as this one outside Canada House, in Woodlands Terrace, Glasgow. January 1957. Photographer: Chris McCrae

The Prince Family, from Wigtown, who were believed to be the largest family ever to emigrate to South Africa up until that time, bid their farewells to Britain. Mr and Mrs Stanley Prince are photographed alongside Lawrence (17), Tony (15), Richard (13), Chris (12), Tim (11), Roger (10), Peter (9), Sally Ann (8), Jennifer (7), Penny (6), Nicholas (4) and Judith (2). February 1957.
Photographer: Unknown

More than 20,000 supporters of CND, the Campaign for Nuclear Disarmament, take part in a 'die-in' in George Square, Glasgow. The protest was over President Reagan's controversial 'Star Wars' missile defence programme and the arrival of Cruise missiles at Greenham. 1983.
Photographer: Unknown

PEOPLE
POWER

CHAPTER TEN

PEOPLE POWER

Any discussion of Glasgow's radical political history is guaranteed to touch on the industrial unrest of 1919. During what was dubbed the Forty-Hours' Strike, the Red Flag famously flew over George Square and tanks were sent in to quell what was suspected to be Bolshevik unrest in Scotland's largest city.

There's no denying the enduring potency of the legend of Red Clydeside. As C. A. Oakley, author of *The Second City*, put it in the mid-1940s:

> For a hundred years Glasgow was regarded as a place with fairly radical political views. After 1919, however, Glasgow had the reputation of leaning towards the more *extreme* left, and not only Great Britain but much of the world began to speak of Red Clydeside.

Glasgow's political history also includes such figures as: Davie Kirkwood, one of the 'wild men of Clydeside', who became a benign peer; Willie Gallacher, once described by Lloyd George as a 'sinister influence' on Clydeside, who became president of the British Communist Party; Jimmy Maxton, the legendary Independent Labour MP for Bridgeton; Manny Shinwell, another Clydeside rebel, who went to jail for incitement to riot and died, a fighter all his days, at the age of 101 in 1986; and John MacLean, venerated by Tommy Sheridan as one of Scotland's greatest socialists, who went to prison five times for his political beliefs and died in 1923, his body having been so ruined by hunger strikes and forced feeding through stomach pumps that he eventually succumbed to pneumonia.

Sometimes overlooked, however, are the events of the General Strike of 1926 and the way they affected Glasgow.

The strike arose at a turbulent time in British politics, a time of trade union militancy, a depressed economy and a fear of Communism. Wages had been slashed and hours increased in the coal industry in 1921 and, when a similar move was tried by the mine-owners in 1925, the unions responded by threatening a general strike. The government stepped in with a nine-month subsidy to boost wages and also established a Royal Commission under Sir Herbert Samuel to look into the coal industry. The following year, Samuel reported and, amongst other things, seemed to accept that pay cuts were inevitable.

The mine owners demanded pay cuts and the re-introduction of an eight-hour day. The miners' leaders rejected this and declined to negotiate. The TUC got involved as the dispute continued to escalate. A lockout began on 30 April and, on 1 May, it was decided at the TUC conference that a general strike would start at midnight on Monday, 3 May.

There was no missing the headline that dominated the *Glasgow Herald* on Tuesday, 4 May. 'GENERAL STRIKE IN PROGRESS', it said and the opening paragraphs confirmed not only that last-minute peace talks had failed but also that the action had already spread far and wide:

> A national strike in vital industries and services – transport, printing trades (including the press), iron and steel, metals and heavy chemicals group, building trades, electricity and gas – began at midnight. It was ascertained on the rising of the House of Commons last night that neither the TUC nor the miners had made any new offer, and therefore the final negotiations ended in failure.
>
> The Government's organisation throughout the country to maintain the distribution of foodstuffs has been perfected and is working smoothly.
>
> Ministers have issued appeals for economy in the consumption of foodstuffs and the use of motor spirit and the telegraph, telephone and postal services . . .

In Glasgow, one of the most immediate and visible impacts was on the newspapers themselves. An Emergency Press was established, combining the *Glasgow Herald*, the *Evening Times* and four other papers.

The first edition, on Wednesday, 5 May, reported that the country as a whole was 'quite calm', though reports from every part of the country indicated that the strike had caused a 'cessation of many industries'. In Glasgow, it was noted, three warships had arrived at the Tail of the Bank. The city's train services were running only a skeleton service.

Thursday's edition, reporting on day two of the strike, led with Prime Minister Stanley Baldwin's appeal to the nation to stand behind the government. The TUC, for its part, was delighted that the response to the strike had not wavered one bit. 'The machine', said its spokesman, 'is working in a manner that has exceeded our expectations.' The government countered by saying that the country remained 'calm and confident', even if a key part of the nation's business was being disrupted.

That same day, however, there was rioting in Glasgow's East End. Some 500 miners from Newton and Cambuslang had arrived in the city to aid pickets at the Ruby Street tramway and together they rushed the depot to evict student volunteers who were rumoured to be inside.

The police repelled the rioters but there were further incidents during the rest of the day. Stones were thrown, windows were smashed, pubs and shops were looted and up to 100 police officers were called out, relying at times on baton charges. One young man was pushed through a broken window and was taken to the Royal Infirmary in a critical condition. Sixty-six people were arrested.

On Friday, day four, another sixty people were arrested as attempts were made in the East End

to hold up traffic, especially bread vans and food lorries. The authorities appealed to civic-minded residents to volunteer as special constables. The Lord Provost and the Sheriff of Lanarkshire urged law-abiding citizens to refrain from congregating in the streets, saying that they 'should avoid the main thoroughfares as much as possible'.

Nationwide, the government insisted that the tasks of distributing food and ensuring supplies of light and power had been maintained. But although it said that no serious disorder had occurred anywhere, the situation was becoming more and more intense.

The strike continued over the weekend and the Monday saw both sides remaining upbeat, with the TUC calling on shipyard workers and marine engineers to join the strike. Three people were killed and thirteen injured when a goods train collided with a passenger train near Edinburgh. On Tuesday, it emerged that peace moves were suddenly in progress with a view to settling the dispute.

On Wednesday came the news that everyone wanted to hear – the strike had been called off, following a meeting in Downing Street with the TUC's General Council. In the Commons, a relieved Baldwin described the peace as a victory for common sense. The TUC, praising the 'magnificent' response to the strike call, said it had called off the action to allow the resumption of talks 'to secure a settlement in the mining industry free and unfettered from either strike or lockout'.

The King sent a swift message of congratulations to the British people. In his private diary, he wrote:

Our old country can well be proud of itself, as during the last nine days there has been a strike in which 4 million men have been affected; not a shot has been fired & no-one killed; it shows what a wonderful people we are.

Workers gather one morning under the chimneys of Babcock and Wilcox, in Renfrew, for an update on their dispute with the company. The strikers decided to return to work pending a works conference to be held later that week. March 1959.
Photographer: Unknown

Men struggle to right a Glasgow bus after it was overturned during riots in the 1926 General Strike. Britain's only general strike lasted for nine days and involved some four million workers, who stopped work in support of the miners' demand for 'not a penny off the pay, not a second on the day'. May 1926. Photographer: Unknown

It wasn't only the men who made their voices heard on the picket lines – these determined women from the Rolls-Royce factory at Hillington were fighting for a wage of nine shillings and sixpence. November 1955. Photographer: Harry Moyes

A worker armed with a placard listens as Labour's technology minister, Tony Benn, addresses a meeting at Upper Clyde Shipbuilders in Clydebank. On this day in 1969, the town witnessed the biggest industrial demonstration in the west of Scotland since the war, with 15,000 downing tools amid fears over local jobs prospects – two local plants had just been condemned to the axe.
February 1969.
Photographer: Jim Hamilton

Red Clydeside. The unforgettable scenes in 1919 in Glasgow's Trongate as tanks, flanked by armed soldiers, make their way down the Trongate en route for various points across the city. They had been dispatched in the aftermath of the Black Friday (or 'Bloody Friday') riot in George Square, when workers, intent on a forty-hour week, clashed with police.

Photographer: Unknown

The Red Flag flies amidst the strikers at a mass rally in George Square during the 1919 unrest. The entire episode – and this photograph in particular – have etched themselves into Glasgow's vivid political history. January, 1919. Photographer: Unknown

Strike leaders Emmanuel Shinwell (left) and Harry Hopkins, two of the leaders of the Clyde Workers' Committee, address a large gathering of workers in George Square in January 1919. Both were among those who were arrested. Shinwell was sentenced to five months' imprisonment. Photographer: Unknown

Bedecked in tartan, draped in the Lion Rampant and equipped with a football rattle, these fans were clearly looking forward to seeing their team take to the field at Wembley. The rattles were popular then and made excessive noise when swung round. Scotland won 3–2 on this occasion, so that rattle must have been heard often. April 1951. Photographer: Unknown

FOOTBALL
FANS

CHAPTER ELEVEN

FOOTBALL FANS

There's a great account by William McIlvanney of the time he and a bunch of other Scotland die-hards travelled overland to Argentina for the 1978 World Cup. Three of them had given up their jobs to go on the trip, which managed to take in not only New York and Mexico City but also Guatemala, El Salvador, Honduras, Nicaragua, Colombia, Peru and finally, almost as an afterthought, Argentina. Jolted along the way by mishap and adventure and by what they had seen of life in the countries they had passed through, the six arrived at their destination in a reflective mood, uncertain where football now stood in their passions.

Their spirits were lifted by the joyous reception they received from the Argentine people but, true to form, the Scottish team, under Ally MacLeod, contrived to let them down again. After watching Scotland lose 3–1 to Peru in the opening game, one of McIlvanney's group left the stadium in tears, giving away his ticket for the next match. When Scotland could only draw that game, against Iran, two others followed suit.

At the final whistle, angry Scotland fans hurled abuse at their own team – McIlvanney described this as 'a moment both futile and angry, like a schizophrenic having an argument with himself. Men who had travelled thousands of miles turned against their own reason for coming and shouted obscenities at it.'

Scotland's inept performance in Argentina (the solitary highlight of their three matches being, of course, Archie Gemmill's wondrous goal against Holland) made many Scots fans wonder why they bothered following the national team – whether, in fact, they were right to invest so much passion in what was, after all, only a game.

Four years later, of course, Scotland was back in the World Cup, this time in Spain, and many of those fans – older and wiser but still optimistic – again went abroad in great numbers. They went to Mexico in 1986, to Italy in 1990, to France in 1998. And they'll be there whenever Scotland next reach the finals of the World Cup, or European Championship. The passion may be dimmed from time to time but it can never be made to disappear entirely.

It's what motivates fans to leave work early in midweek to drive 100 miles to watch their team take part in an end-of-season game that almost redefines the word 'inconsequential'. It's what courses through the veins of Gretna's fans when they turned up at Hampden for the Scottish Cup against Hearts, many of them wondering if they were in the middle of an elaborate dream. It's why Billy Connolly likes few things better than to watch Celtic in action and why Sir Sean Connery, a man who had previously been spotted at both Ibrox and Celtic Park, to say

nothing of having watched Hibs and Hearts when he was growing up in Edinburgh, was happy to reveal that he has followed unfashionable Dunfermline all his life.

Such passion is hard to define but you know it when you see it.

It's there in men such as Motherwell FC's veteran chaplain, Rev. Dr James Martin, a walking encyclopaedia on the history of the club who, each Tuesday, jogs round the ground he knows almost as well as he knows his own house. One of his daughters was rumoured to have banned him from travelling too far afield but he got round that by going to away games on the team bus. 'He's part of the club family,' said Terry Butcher, Motherwell's manager at the time.

And it's there in fans of perennial underachievers like East Stirling, a team who have had the label of 'worst football team in Britain' for so long that they could almost copyright it. Indeed, the label formed part of the title of a recent book about the Shire, an account of a season spent by the author, Jeff Connor, at Firs Park in Falkirk. Having spent the first nine years of my life in a house just across from the ground, I've always had a soft spot for the club and for its fans. Supporting East Stirling – a 'raddled institution', in Connor's words – requires fortitude and dedication but there's surely passion for the game there, too.

At the other end of the scale, there was that May night in Seville, in 2003, when Celtic heroically tried to win the UEFA Cup. An estimated 80,000 Celtic fans arrived in Spain from all over the world. The pride that all of them felt for their team, even when the game ended in defeat, was a moving reminder of the role that football has in their lives. As Celtic fan Elaine C. Smith wrote afterwards:

> As a nation we tend towards the pessimistic, the navel-gazing, the insecurity and the lack of self-belief yet, here in May 2003 . . . Scottish Celtic fans were allowed to dream. Not only that, most of the nation were sharing the dream.

Can Scotland under Walter Smith reach the finals of Euro 2008 in Austria and Switzerland? It would be nice to think that they could but the only thing that is certain is that, wherever they play, the Tartan Army – 'the most bizarre fan-base in football', according to Stuart Cosgrove – will be there. The hard lessons of the past have been learned and we no longer indulge in the kind of unhinged optimism that attended the World Cup squad's noisy departure for Argentina, back in 1978. We're more pragmatic now and we half-expect to witness yet another grand Scottish failure. But the passion and the hope that, against all the odds, we might actually achieve something still make the Army, again in Cosgrove's words, an 'awesome sight'.

In the meantime, the pictures in this section are proof of what the late Cliff Hanley once said: 'The basic truth, of course, is that our great institution of football isn't really about players. It's about fans and their fine madness, and the game itself is just a pretext for that madness.'

'I'm sorry sir, we're arresting you for being in possession of an offensive jacket!' A Scotland fan leads these two policemen a merry dance during a Scotland–England clash at Hampden Park, May 1974. Scotland won the match 2–0. Photographer: Unknown

'Did you say this was a two-legged affair?' A Rangers fan suffering from a cut foot is wheeled away by ambulancemen but the fan doesn't let a small inconvenience like this detract from his enjoyment of the Old Firm New Year's game. January 1969.
Photographer: James Millar

Hats off to Scotland and don't forget the cigar! Scotland fans all decked out in tartan leave Central Station in Glasgow, bound for Wembley and the annual England–Scotland fixture. The Wembley clash resulted in a 2–2 draw. April 1953.
Photographer: George Ashton

So this is what they mean by getting capped for Scotland – crowds of fans arrive at Hampden for a big game with bunnets galore and the occasional bowler and trilby, with scarcely a bare head to be seen anywhere. Photographer: Unknown

The reel thing – two Scotland supporters give an impromptu display of Highland dancing in Frankfurt during the national team's heroic efforts in the World Cup Finals. June 1974. Photographer: Unknown

Two police officers have their hands full trying to close a gate that was being breached by fans desperate to get into Cathkin Park for a Third Lanark–Rangers match. August 1961. Photographer: Unknown

Bhoys jumping for joy. Celtic supporters, perched directly behind the goalposts, leap into the air after John McPhail scores the winning goal in their Scottish Cup tie against Hearts at Tynecastle. McPhail himself would get the winner in the final against Motherwell. 1951.

Photographer: Unknown

Getting into the match mood, William Davidson of Welwyn Garden City arrives in Glasgow to support Scotland against the Auld Enemy. Unfortunately it was a long trip for William, without much to show for it – Scotland lost 2–1 to England. April 1952.
Photographer: George Ashton

Members of a formation dance team called the Rockets display a new-fangled dance at the Albert Ballroom. The dance was called the twist, and it would prove to be immensely popular. The Rockets were good – they had once appeared on *Sunday Night at the London Palladium*, a top TV show of the era. April 1965.

Photographer: Peter Turner

DANCING

CHAPTER TWELVE

DANCING

Once, decades ago, they meant something, but not now. Billy McGregor and his Gaybirds. Dr Crock and his Crackpots. Harry Gold and his Big New Orchestra. The Palais Glide, the Black Bottom, the Astoria, the F+F, the Playhouse. All of these bands, dances and venues date from the time when going dancing meant stepping into a proper dance-hall and not, as now, stumbling into a dark, cavernous club with a DJ playing the latest garage, trance or house.

The novelist Zoë Strachan, who dug deep into a largely vanished world while researching her novel, *Spin Cycle*, believes that dance-halls, together with cinemas:

offered excitement and fun, the tantalising possibility of romance, but most of all they offered escape. Escape from the daily grind, and the fantasy, for whole evenings at a time, of a glamorous other life.

The more research Zoë did:

the greater the significance of the dancing was revealed to be, until it seemed that every bus conductress spent her working day with her curlers tucked under her headscarf, every factory worker rushed home to glue on her false eyelashes and every teacher practised her jiving in front of the mirror in anticipation of the band on the revolving stage at the Locarno. In particular, stories abounded of women who took off their wedding rings, suggesting that the girls' night out was alive and adulterous.

But not universal – not if Andy Cameron's recollection of the Dennistoun Palais being known as 'Knockback City' is any guide.

To take one week at random – the first week in April, 1954 – you and your mates could turn up at the Plaza, the Astoria in Sauchiehall Street (with its Nylon Gift Night and Beat-the-Band contest on Tuesdays), the Dennistoun Palais, Green's Playhouse ('Betty Taylor, Jon Clark, Margaret Rose with Harry Gold and his Big New Orchestra'), the Barrowland, the Berkeley or the West End at Charing Cross ('The Dancers' Rendezvous').

But there were more ballrooms than just those large, well-known ones in the city centre. Others included South Govan Town Hall ('music by the Merry Macs'), the Eastmuir Masonic on Shettleston Road, Rutherglen Town Hall with Dave Scott's Night Hawks, Whiteinch Burgh Hall,

Tollcross Co-op Hall, Breslin's in Bridgeton, Syd Low's Old-Time Dancing Club at Royal Crescent on Sauchiehall Street, the Over-25s Central Dance Studio Club in Bath Street. And so on and on, like a never-ending dance.

It was no wonder that, when the New Savoy Cinema reopened five years later as the Majestic, the *Glasgow Herald* observed:

> Glasgow is the dancing-est place in all Britain, and no one seems to know why . . . While cinemas have withered, the dancing industry has gone from strength to strength. Certainly, nothing looks like stopping it in Glasgow, while plans for two more halls are already in hand.

Musician Len Skeat, one of Britain's best-known double bassists, played with Bill Shearer's group at the opening of the new hall, which soon became known as the 'Magic Stick' to Glaswegians. Len was just twenty-two at the time. 'Somewhere in my scrapbook,' he says, 'I have a very frayed old picture of the event. I was there for a week or a fortnight or so. The place was packed and the atmosphere for the dancing was absolutely wonderful.'

Another man with fond memories of the halls is Bill Anderson, of Cadder, Glasgow. It was in December of 1943 that he met the woman who was to become the love of his life. 'The dance-halls were marvellous and the dancing was absolutely magic,' says Bill, now eighty-five. He continues:

> During the war, I would be home on leave from the Royal Navy and would go to the Playhouse for its afternoon dance and that's where I met Nancy. I immediately knew she was the one for me. We just clicked and we seemed to fall in love and that was us. We had a glorious time dancing and, when I went back to my ship, we'd write to each other every day. When I got more leave, we'd spend it together, too.

Eleven months after their first encounter, Bill and Nancy decided to get engaged. 'We traipsed up and down and looked in many jewellers' shops but couldn't find a ring. In those days, the selection and the quality were limited, which was not surprising because there was a war on.'

In February 1945, Bill found himself at Yalta, in the Crimea, where Churchill, Roosevelt and Stalin held a summit meeting. Stalin, Roosevelt and Churchill agreed to split Germany into four zones of occupation. Late one night, Winston came down a jetty on his way to Bill's ship, and it was so dark that the Glasgow man needed a big lamp to show him down the stairs.

When Bill came home the following month, he and Nancy were married within three days by special licence.

We had only spent thirty-nine days together since December 1943 but we never doubted it would last. We continued to go the dancing – to the Albert, the Berkeley, the Green's Playhouse, the Plaza, the Locarno – these were marvellous, marvellous days.

We didn't drink in these days. There was no drink in the dance-halls anyway – you went there to dance. The band would start at 7.30 and you'd be there before they came on and it would be dancing, dancing all night. There'd be bands at the Playhouse like Oscar Rabin, Joe Loss, Lou Preger, The Squadronnaires. The bands would play the Playhouse for maybe three weeks and then go somewhere else.

At the Plaza you'd have Jack Chapman, who was also in the Albert. Harry Margolis was in the Plaza as well – I thought of him when I read that the Plaza is being turned into flats. George Elrick and his band used to play the Dennistoun Palais, a massive hall. At the Locarno, they had the turntable – a big band would play on it and then the table would swivel round and a smaller band would come in and play for an hour.

You'd wrap your black patent shoes in brown paper with an elastic band round them and, when you got to the hall, you'd go down to the cloakroom and change into them. They'd get all tatty but you loved them because they were so good for your dancing. The men were always in suits and the women were always in nice dresses. I used to have two pairs of made-to-measure trousers – one for walking out in, the other for when I went dancing. You needed two pairs because the stuff they put on the dance-floor would come off on them.

I think it was the Swinging Sixties that changed dancing as we knew it but it never changed anything for Nancy and me – we continued dancing all our lives. I'm not being boastful but people always said we were good dancers.

Sadly, Nancy passed away early on 7 October 2005, after one last night's dancing.

We were together for sixty-two years and still liked dancing until the end. On the Saturday night we went to a Second World War Veterans' dance in the Central Hotel, with Harry Margolis and his band. We danced all night, and had a marvellous night.

The following day, Nancy slipped and fell. She died less than a week later. 'We started in the dancing,' says Bill, 'and our last night was spent at the dancing.'

'Your taxi awaits, sir.' The exterior of the 'Denny Palais', the
Dennistoun Palais. Rebuilt and reopened in 1938 after a fire, it was the
city's largest dance-hall, with a capacity of 1,800. It's been claimed
that, if you went round the dance-floor ten times, you'd walked a mile.
Note the uniformed doorman! 1957. Photographer: John MacKay

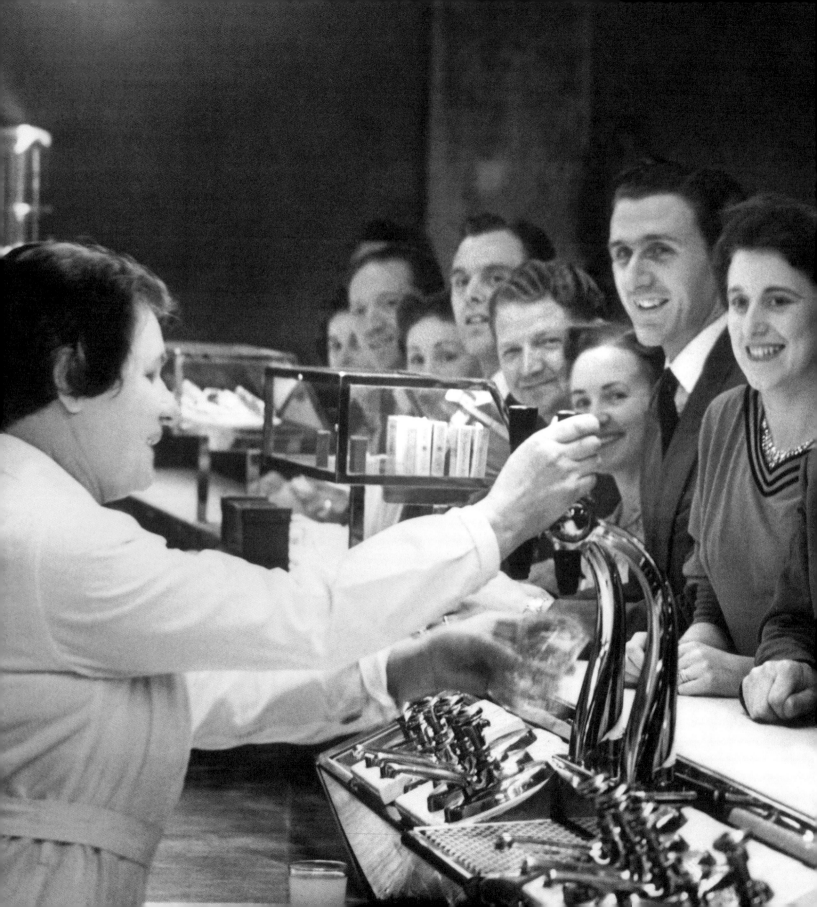

Time for a refreshing break at the
Dennistoun Palais. Smartly dressed
dancers line up at the self-service café
at the popular Saturday night venue.
April 1954.
Photographer: John Mackay

At the height of the dancehall era, The Albert, in Bath Street, was hugely popular. It was opened by the Warren family in 1905 and, in the 1920s, its dancers took enthusiastically to the Charleston and other dance crazes. The Albert suffered a blaze in the early 1950s but quickly reopened for business. January 1962.
Photographer: James Millar

The inimitable facade of the Locarno, in Sauchiehall Street. It was opened in 1926 and, within two years, was staging the first Scottish Professional Dancing Championships. For decades, the Locarno was one of the city's best-loved dance-halls. American servicemen, stationed over here during the Second World War, flocked here in search of fun and companionship. July 1938.
Photographer: Unknown

'Wonder what time Santa arrives?' Two Glasgow children wait up – probably long past their bedtime we suspect – for a certain bearded gentleman to come huffing and puffing down their chimney. Best wait until the fire goes out then! December 1959.
Photographer: James Millar

CHRISTMAS

CHAPTER THIRTEEN

CHRISTMAS

Willie Gall, the *Evening Times'* legendary cartoonist, liked his Christmas – and he liked doing cartoons about the festivities. There's the one with the unshaven layabout, still in his vest, with a tattoo on his forearm and a fag in his mouth, clutching his present from his wife and complaining to her about it, 'Jist whit ah needed, an executive bleedin' briefcase!' Or the one with the two women who meet in a department store, laden with Christmas goods. 'Ma man's no' buyin' me a fur coat this year. Whit's your man no' buyin' ye?'

In the *Evening Times* of Christmas half-a-century ago – December 1956 – there's another timely cartoon. A woman in a card shop says, 'As it's no' the card that counts, but the spirit in which it is sent, hiv ye ony at tuppence?'

Such cartoons remind you that, with Christmas, as in many other areas, the more things change, the more they stay the same.

You could argue that Christmas today has become a bloated, cynical and vastly commercial enterprise – but, as in 1956, we buy each other nice presents, crowd round the box with the family and eat as much nice food as we can lay our hands on.

Back then, Glaswegians had responded to 'post early' appeals from the Post Office, sending out 12.7 million letters and cards. The shops and the stores, meanwhile, had been trying to shift as much as they could in the run-up to the big day, taking out big adverts to push everything from beaver lamb coats ('only 25 guineas') to Terylene stockings, Crombies (luxury pile overcoats), twin sets in Orlon or pure wool, duffle coats, football jerseys, towel gift sets and books.

Then, as now, once all the gifts had been unwrapped – the clothes, the toys, the home-wares, the vinyl records (how many people that Christmas received a copy of Mel Torme's new album or the new single by a promising new name, 'the singing bus driver', Matt Monro?) – the family would gather round the TV set. If they were lucky that year, they'd be watching one of the new models, like HMV's 21-inch High Fidelity TV (129 guineas for the console model but ninety-eight guineas if you were happy to settle for a table model).

That said, there wasn't much to watch on TV that particular Tuesday – commercial television hadn't penetrated this far north yet. The schedule began with an hour-long *Family Service* until noon. At 2.55, the Duke of Edinburgh addressed the nation from the Royal Yacht *Britannia*, giving way within five minutes to his wife, at Sandringham, who urged Britons to 'make room at the inn' for refugees 'driven from their own lands by war or violence'.

And on the schedule went – *The Variety Theatre of China*, then *The Grand Circus from Paris*, *Puss in Boots* (a filmed story narrated by Johnny Morris), *The Lone Ranger* film, Max Wall in *Ice Crackers*, then sport and weather, followed by act two of the *Marriage of Figaro*, then the news, then *Christmas Disneyland*, then a panto show, a comedy, then *Music for You*, followed by news and weather at 11.15, then closedown. Between them, the radio stations – Scottish, Third, Light and Luxembourg – could offer more variety.

Even better, there was no shortage of things to do in and around town. There were Christmas Carnival Dances at the Dennistoun Palais and the Astoria ballroom in Sauchiehall Street, a carnival and circus at the Kelvin Hall. Frank Weir – 'The Pied Piper of the 20th Century!' – and his 'terrific orchestra' were at Green's Playhouse. The same venue had screenings of Disney's *Lady and the Tramp*. Green's Bedford, at Eglinton Street, had Gordon MacRae and Sheree North in *The Best Things in Life Are Free*.

There were movies at the ABCs Regal and Coliseum, at the Gaumont and the New Savoy (Norman Wisdom in *Up in the World*), at the Rose Street Cosmo (which also had its annual Christmas cinema for kids). The X-rated *Clochemerle* was at the NewCine in Sauchiehall Street and Anthony Quayle was in *The Battle of the River Plate* at the Renfield Street Odeon.

Out in the suburbs, there were plenty of films to catch, whether it was at the ABC in Govanhill, the ABC Toledo in Muirend, the Vogue in Possilpark or the New Star in Maryhill. The State, at King's Park, had Glenn Ford in *Appointment in Honduras*.

The theatres weren't exactly dark, either. There was *Alice in Wonderland* at the Citz and Chic Murray, Duncan Macrae, Jack Anthony and Robert Wilson in *We're Joking*, at the Empire. The Pavilion had Jack Milroy in *Puss in Boots* and the New Empress was running Billy Risk in *Yuletide Frolics* ('The Only Theatre in Glasgow with a Weekly Change of Programme'). Jack Radcliffe was in *Robinson Crusoe*, at the Royal, but his co-star Harry Gordon was temporarily indisposed due to flu (he'd been laid up for ten months the previous year with a heart attack) and his place had been taken by Radcliffe's 'feed', Helen Norman.

At the Alhambra, Jimmy Logan, Rikki Fulton and Kenneth McKellar were running riot in *Babes in the Wood*. Logan had already been on TV that Christmas Eve with his *Loganberry Pie* show, in which he and his co-stars, not to mention Rangers star George Young, Celtic's Bobby Evans and boxer Dick McTaggart (winner of an Olympic gold at Melbourne that summer) had entertained kids from city hospitals and homes.

Otherwise, the city was fairly quiet. Football fans had had their pre-Christmas fun that Saturday – Celtic had beaten Airdrie 7–3 away, Rangers had lost 3–2 at Kilmarnock, Partick Thistle had beaten St Mirren 2–0 and Hearts were top of the league.

But certain people were still working that Tuesday. At Glasgow Maternity Hospital, staff welcomed their first Christmas babies, twin girls born to a Rutherglen mum. Newspaper reporters and photographers visited the hospital to get words and pictures for the Boxing Day paper.

Up on Ben Nevis, a search had begun for four English climbers who'd been out on the upper slopes since early on Christmas morning. Police were investigating an overnight break-in and theft of 4000 unused petrol coupons from an engineering company's premises in Farnell Street at Round Toll.

And, up near Campbeltown, ten bus passengers, one of them a woman of seventy, who'd left Glasgow on Christmas Day at 3 p.m., just as the Queen was starting her televised speech from Sandringham, were recovering from a nightmare journey, having been stranded by snowdrifts thirteen miles from their destination. A kindly local resident had given them blankets and hot drinks, and the passengers eventually reached Campbeltown on Boxing Day morning – twenty-one hours after setting out.

'That's a taxi behind you, m'am, if only you cared to look!' This pedestrian in Orchard Park, Giffnock, prefers to trudge through the snow rather than flag down the taxi. Maybe her home was only yards away though. December 1959.
Photographer: Harry Moulson

Christmas shopping at the old Wylie Hills department store in Buchanan Street, Glasgow, 1955 – it was one of the many famous names that helped make the street a Mecca for shoppers from Glasgow and from further afield.
Photographer: Harry Moyes

The Duke of Wellington
statue – minus, for once,
its traffic cone – gazes at
cars and passers-by during
a wintry afternoon in
January 1955.
Photographer: Dunky
Stewart

An evocative shot, from half a century ago, of the snow-bound junction of
Argyle Street, Oswald Street and Hope Street, with trams and trolleybuses
delivery lorries and a lone man tugging a cart behind him, his head bent
against the elements. January 1955. Photographer: John MacKay

George Square really looks magical at Christmas time, its statues covered in snow and its lamp posts
strung with lights. This picture was taken more than forty years ago but, at first glance, could have
been taken at any time in more recent years. December 1962. Photographer: Unknown

Winter trees form an
archway for children
playing in the snow at
Saracen Street,
Possilpark, Glasgow.
February 1950.
Photographer: Bert
Paterson

The statue of King William III in Cathedral Square, Glasgow, first erected in 1735 outside the Tolbooth, takes on a forbidding look under its layer of snow on a winter's afternoon in February 1942. Photographer: Dunky Stewart

Back in the days when Buchanan Street still saw traffic, this was how it looked at Christmas time, forty-five years ago. The twinkling festive lights are reflected in the polished metalwork of the cars. November 1961. Photographer: Arthur Kinloch

Snow falls gently on a silent
Garnet Street, Glasgow,
during the winter of 1952.
These snow-covered
housewives must have been
chilled to the bone to say the
least but they still managed to
raise a wry smile for the
photographer.
January 1952.
Photographer: George Ashton

Snow has transformed this everyday scene in
St Enoch Square, Glasgow, into something
memorable. Old-fashioned cars lie under a
blanket of snow while, in front of them, a man
leads his horse through the freezing slush.
January 1952. Photographer: Dunky Stewart

A winter's postcard scene as two teams, each
consisting of 1300 curlers, take to the ice on
Lake of Menteith for the Bonspiel in 1979. The
previous event had been held in 1963.
Photographer: Arthur Kinloch